A CHILD SHALL LEAD THEM

A Guide to Celebrating the Word With Children

Editor/Contributing Author
GERARD A. POTTEBAUM

Contributing Authors
SISTER PAULE FREEBURG, D.C.
JOYCE M. KELLEHER

TREEHAUS COMMUNICATIONS, INC.
P.O. Box 249 • Loveland, Ohio 45140

The scripture readings adapted for children
and quoted throughout this book are taken
from the SUNDAY *Lectionary for Children,*
copyrighted 1989-90-91 by Forum Katecheticum.

The music for children is by
Christopher Walker and
copyrighted as indicated where
the musical notations appear.

Library of Congress Catalog No. 92-062896

ISBN 0-929496-65-5

A CHILD SHALL LEAD THEM

Dedication

In grateful memory of
CHRISTIANE BRUSSELMANS
November 1, 1930 - October 29, 1991

CONTENTS

Introduction

This is what the prophet Isaiah said to the people of Israel:

"A child will be born in the family of Jesse.
This child will be filled with the Spirit of God,
the spirit of wisdom and understanding,
the spirit of strength and truth,
the spirit of knowledge and love of God.
The one who is coming will not judge
by what others say or by what people look like
but will judge the poor with justice and fairness.
Then the wolf will live with the lamb.
The leopard and the goat will eat together.
The bear and the lion will be at peace,
and a little child will lead them all.
This child will be a sign for all the world.
Then no one will hurt others anymore
because everyone will know God."

(Isaiah 11:1-10)

Christians believe that the child of whom Isaiah speaks in this colorful image of God's Kingdom is Jesus. The description, however, also complements the life story of Moses, who, plucked from the river bushes, grew up to lead Israel to freedom from slavery in Egypt. In either case, is it mere coincidence that Isaiah should speak of one who liberates people as *a child* rather than as an adult?

Recall, too—as overly familiar as it may seem to us—what Jesus himself said:

"Amen I say to you,
  whoever does not receive
  the kingdom of God like a child
  shall not enter it."
                    (*Mark* 10:15)

Reflect also on the answer Jesus gave when his disciples asked him, "Who is the greatest in the kingdom of heaven?"

"And calling to him a child,
  he put the child in the midst of them, and said,
    'Truly, I say to you, unless you turn
    and become like children,
    you will never enter the kingdom of heaven.
    Those who humble themselves like this child,
    are the greatest in the kingdom of heaven.
    Whoever receives one such child
    in my name receives me;
    but whoever causes one of these little ones
    who believe in me to sin,
    it would be better for that person
    to have a great millstone
    fastened around the neck and
    to be drowned in the depth of the sea.' "
                    (*Matthew* 18: 1- 6)

Such biblical texts are strong evidence of the central role children play in the gospel of Jesus. Equally important, they reveal Jesus' attitude toward the place of children in the community. Moreover, they offer insight into the quality and character of Jesus' own spiritual life. When Jesus prayed, he declared: "I thank you, Father, Lord of heaven and earth, that you have hidden these things from the wise and understanding and revealed them to children." (*Matthew* 11:25).

Jesus recognized the spiritual life of children is uncluttered and close to God. For Jesus, the child—not the adult—is his primary model of spirituality.

So often—too often—we parents and parish leaders forget that children already enjoy a spiritual life—not without the influences of socialization but also not without its own mysterious and original power. Although well-intentioned, we approach children as if their souls were some kind of empty container, given by God for us to fill with the truths of faith and certain moral codes to guide their behavior. This is not to say that we have nothing to teach children. The point is: we sometimes get in our own way—and in God's way. Jesus did *not* tell us to teach children to be like us; rather, Jesus told us adults that *it is we who have something to learn from children.*

In his book *The Children's God* (University of Chicago Press, 1986), David Heller reported that, based on his research, religion teachers and parents often block unconventional or noninstitutional views of God and thereby discourage children from their own original beliefs and discovery. I have found his observation supported again and again by stories adults have told me about experiences in their early childhood that continue to affect the quality and character of their spiritual lives as adults.

One lady, for example, reported that when she was 3 or 4 years old, she returned home from church one Sunday after mass and excitedly ran to the kitchen to get juice and bread so that she could celebrate mass like the priest. Upon discovering what she was doing, her parents told her, apparently in no uncertain terms, that little girls could not and should not do that. Only men who were ordained priests could change bread and wine into the body and blood of Christ.

On another occasion, a man described the image that he, when still a very young child, held of his father: a large and mighty man, more powerful than anyone in the whole world. One night the child entered his father's bedroom where he found his father kneeling in prayer. In this otherwise ordinary experience, the child felt a presence even more powerful than his father, the hidden but nonetheless real presence of God. The discovery still stirs wonder and awe in this person's spiritual life.

What does any of this have to do, you might ask, with celebrating the Liturgy of the Word with children? I'm sure you can make any number of connections, not the least of which includes the child's capacity to read symbolic action and the impact of ritual-making on a child's spirituality.

Aside from these, I want to focus on still another related observation: *attitude—our attitude* toward children and how we perceive of their spiritual lives, their sense of God's action in their lives, and how we might nurture and be enriched ourselves by the life of the Spirit in children. When we can recognize and acknowledge, as Jesus did, the unique expression of God's presence in children, then we can celebrate the word in a way that is meaningful to them and respectful of their spirituality. By so doing, it is *we* who will discover the wisdom and understanding that God has already revealed to them: the kingdom of surprise and wonder, where lions and lambs are friends.

In the reign of God, children are not second-class citizens, to be seen and not heard. The kingdom, as Jesus said, belongs to them. They—and those who become like them—are the gatekeepers. This relationship between children and God should tell us something about the way we "teach" children to pray either in private or in public worship.

We "teach" our children to pray when we ourselves pray in such a way that they can pray with us. This does not mean children adapt to accommodate us. Rather, our prayer is guided by the spiritual relationship that children—and those who are like them—enjoy with God. So, too, we celebrate the Liturgy of the Word in such a way that children can celebrate with us. In other words, our celebration should reflect and be guided by the spiritual relationship children enjoy with God as keepers of the kingdom.

The question is: how well do our parish liturgies show respect for children and draw upon their grace—the life of the Spirit in them—to nourish and guide the spiritual growth of the entire community? Our language gives us away when we speak, for example, of the Liturgy of the Word *for* children, as if it were something different *for* adults. It is important to remember when we celebrate the Liturgy of the Word with children, we serve not only the needs and rights of children to hear God's word in language they can understand, we also serve the spiritual needs of the entire community.

If we humble ourselves enough to let the child, of whom Isaiah so eloquently spoke, *lead us*, then we just may be in for a wonderful surprise. We may find through our children what we thought they would find through us. It is in this spirit and with this attitude that we write *A CHILD SHALL LEAD THEM: A Guide to Celebrating the Word With Children.*

Congregations can celebrate the word with children in a variety of ways. *One way* is to invite the children to a celebration that is an extension of the main assembly's celebration. This style of celebration is the focus of this book.

You might liken this style of celebrating the word with children to the way a growing family—or group of families—manages family gatherings. The adults often eat at one table with the little children who are still too young to feed themselves. As the family grows in number and the children grow in age, the children eat with their older brothers, sisters, cousins or friends at another table where they are served by adults and eat the same food as the adults, but enjoy their own conversations.

After a time, when they have grown still older, they return to the larger table where they become part of the gathering of adults and the new family additions—who are, by now, grandchildren. The growing children do not feel any less a part of the family as they move from one table to the next. On the contrary, the movement takes on a symbolic, ritual character that gives recognition to each child's evolving place in the family. Often, as the meal progresses and the very little children have finished eating, the older children rejoin the adults at the larger table, or become involved in games with each other and the adults.

Such gatherings of individual families or groups of families, with their attending customs and family menus and recipes, give children their identity—not only as a McCarthy or Schmidt or Wong or Cywinski or Rivers but also as *Kathleen* McCarthy or *Willie* Schmidt or *Zenia* Wong or *Donald* Cywinski or *Marie* Rivers. We do not become members of our families first by studying our family rituals and customs. Nor are we required to know certain things before we can participate. From the beginning, we simply do what everyone normally does when they gather.

The parish gathering, with its attending rituals, also gives us and our children identity with Christ's life. We learn that identity not so much by formal instruction but by gathering with the community, sharing in its rituals and living the community's life in Christ. That is why it is so important that we *not* turn liturgy into learning experiences but that we celebrate well together, listen to God's word, and respond with good works.

We need, therefore, to keep in mind that the Liturgy of the Word with children is not intended to be a learning experience—though it has its own formative influence on children. Rather, the Liturgy of the Word is the ritual celebration of God's own presence with us. *God's own presence*: what an awesome influence!

The Liturgy of the Word with children is more properly identified with worship rather than as another form or part of parish religious education or catechetical programs. Moreover, as an integral part of parish worship, recognizing the place of children in our liturgical celebrations is a parish priority. Without such recognition and respect, our sacramental preparation programs, catechetical instruction, and religious education efforts—whether lectionary-based or otherwise—are like so many dinghies adrift at sea with neither mother ship nor harbor in sight—and, little hope for homecoming.

As you read the chapters of this book, you will find

these two points of view or attitudes apparent throughout. First, that *our children already enjoy a spiritual life that is the model for all who wish to enter God's kingdom.* Second, that *the Liturgy of the Word with children is worship—the ritual celebration of God's presence in the word.*

We want also to emphasize a third point: simplicity. We risk communicating the notion that celebrating the word with children is complicated when we spend so much verbiage on the significance of inviting the children to celebrate, the way we handle the book, listening to what the children have heard God say to them, incorporating music, creating a setting conducive to prayer, and all the liturgical refinements. Celebrating the word is not complicated. It is very simple. Moreover, it is in their simplicity that our ritual gestures, proclamation of the word, music-making and environmental effects succeed in awakening a profound sense of God's presence in our humble gatherings.

Simply put: it is the Spirit alive in the children, our love for one another, and our belief in God's presence in the word upon which everything else depends. We hope the discussion questions at the end of each chapter will serve you well in developing a parish team whose style of celebrating the word with children achieves a graceful simplicity characteristic of Jesus' own spirituality.

The ideas and suggestions that you will find here come not only from the authors, but from the experience of parishes throughout the country.

Sister Paule Freeburg has celebrated the word with children in a variety of parishes and parochial schools. She will be the first to admit that her sense of God's presence in the word reawakens each time she gathers with children and listens to what they have heard God say to them. These children share in her contribution to this book, specifically in chapters 8, 9, and 12. Sister Paule, of course, also brings her scholarly and personal love of the scriptures, as the primary author of the adaptation of the scriptures for children in the SUNDAY *Lectionary.*

Joyce Kelleher has 17 years' experience as a volunteer catechist and five as a parish director of religious education. She is currently the Director, Office of Initiation and Spiritual Formation, for the Diocese of Greensburg, Pennsylvania. She is one of the leaders in the development of the catechumenate and in recognizing the formative influence of ritual in Christian initiation. Her contribution to this book reflects that experience and vision, particularly in chapters 2, 3, 4, and 6.

Finally, as general editor and co-author, I have to acknowledge that, although I have been involved for over 30 years in the liturgical and catechetical movements, my focus during the last few years on celebrating the word with children and my involvement as publisher of *SUNDAY*, grows out of my friendship of almost 30 years and professional association with Christiane Brusselmans. Those who know Christiane through her workshops, publications, or proddings, should know that this book, too, is not without her influence. That is why we dedicate it to her memory on this first anniversary of her death.

Gerard A. Pottebaum
October 29, 1992

Chapter 1

WHAT IS THE CELEBRATION
OF THE WORD
WITH CHILDREN?

The celebration of the word with children—or, Liturgy of the Word—is part of the eucharistic liturgy. It follows the norms established in 1973 by the *Directory for Masses with Children* which is a supplement to the "General Instruction of the Revised Roman Missal," published in 1969.

"The *Directory* is concerned with children who have not yet entered the period of pre-adolescence. It does not speak directly of children who are physically or mentally retarded because a broader adaptation is sometimes necessary for them. Nevertheless, the (*Directory's*) norms may also be applied to the retarded, with the necessary changes" (Paragraph 6).

In its introduction, the *Directory* clearly states that "a special difficulty arises from the fact that liturgical celebrations, especially the eucharist, cannot fully exercise their innate pedagogical force upon children. Although the mother tongue may now be used at Mass, still the words and signs have not been sufficiently adapted to the capacity of children.

"In fact, even in daily life children cannot always understand everything that they experience with adults, and they easily become weary. It cannot be expected, moreover, that everything in the liturgy will always be

intelligible to them. Nonetheless, we may fear spiritual
harm if over the years children repeatedly experience in
the Church things that are scarcely comprehensible to
them...." (Paragraph 2).

The authors of the *Directory* go on to say that the
intent, however, is not to create a new rite for children. It
is, rather, a matter of "retaining, shortening, or omitting
some elements or of making a better selection of texts"
(First Synod of Bishops, Liturgy: *Notitiae*, 3 [1967] 368).

In discussing Masses with adults in which children also
participate, the authors warn that great care needs to be
taken so that "children do not feel neglected because of
their inability to participate or to understand what
happens and what is proclaimed in the celebration....
Sometimes, moreover, it will perhaps be appropriate, if the
physical arrangements and circumstances of the
community permit, to celebrate the Liturgy of the Word,
including a homily, with the children in a separate area
that is not too far removed. Then, before the eucharistic
liturgy begins, the children are led to the place where the
adults have meanwhile been celebrating their own Liturgy
of the Word" (Paragraph 17). This guide deals specifically
with this situation in which children leave the general
assembly for a special celebration for children.

The celebration of the word with children, therefore,
follows the same structure as the Liturgy of the Word with
the general assembly of Christians. The complete
structure is as follows:

1. The Gathering Rites
2. The Invitation to Celebrate the Word
3. Procession with the Book of Readings
4. Welcoming
5. First Reading
6. Response
7. Gospel Acclamation
8. Gospel
9. Reflection on Readings
10. Profession of Faith (optional)

11. Prayer of the Faithful (optional)
12. Return of Children to Main Assembly

We need not include each of these parts in every celebration. However, we should not omit consistently one or another of them. While the *Directory* recommends that we judiciously omit and adapt portions of the rite when necessary, we are not to change or omit certain elements. As we review each of these components, we will remain faithful to the principles described in the *Directory*.

1. The Gathering Rite

When the children go to mass, they first gather with the entire congregation, young and old. Everyone participates in these introductory or Gathering Rite up to and including the Opening Prayer. The children participate in these rites because they are part of the whole community and need to know they belong to the larger parish family.

In Chapter 5 we will discuss in greater length the significance of gathering the children with the larger community, rather than simply having the children, upon their arrival at church, go directly to a separate space.

2. Invitation to Celebrate the Word

After the Opening Prayer, the priest gives the children recognition by inviting them to join with the leader of the word. The priest may say something like this: "I invite the children to come forward and join in the procession for their celebration of the word."

The priest may then present the Sunday lectionary for children to a designated child or to the adult leader, with a gesture of commissioning or blessing. The priest may pray with the community over the children with a statement such as: "May the Spirit of God open the ears and hearts of our children—and of us all—as we proclaim God's presence in the word."

In Chapter 5 we will discuss in more detail this part of the rite and deal with some of the concerns about

separating children from the larger community. The
important point is that the children need to be recognized
as a significant part of the larger community. Their separate
gathering is not to be handled in such a way as to convey to
either the adults or the children that now the lesser
members of the community are being removed or dismissed.

3. Procession with the Book of Readings
The Sunday lectionary for children is an important
sign. It is a primary focal point of the celebration of the
word. It symbolizes God's presence in our lives throughout
human history. It symbolizes our inheritance of God's
covenant of love for us. The book should be carried
reverently and in a way that the children can see it is special.
Servers carrying lighted candles may walk on either
side of the book. Another server, carrying a processional
cross, may lead the way. Children who wish to participate
may follow.
The entire community may join with the children in
singing an appropriate antiphon or psalm response. The
object here is to center the attention and create the mood
for both the children and those remaining in the general
assembly to hear God's word proclaimed.
Some liturgists observe that the children's procession
at this point in the celebration risks interrupting the flow
of the movement from the Gathering Rite to the Liturgy of
the Word. On the other hand, other liturgists observe
that, to the contrary, the procession can help to *heighten*
the assembly's anticipation for the celebration of the word.
We may take a lesson from the ritual practice in the
Eastern Rite, where the proclamation of the word is
preceded by a procession with the scriptures through the
assembly, thereby making an even more dramatic gesture
to elevate the congregation's sense of respect for God's
presence in the word.

4. Welcoming
When the children arrive in the place of celebration,
they need to be re-gathered and a transition needs to be

made between the ending of the procession and the proclamation of the word. This is done by welcoming.

We encourage you to use music during the procession; it helps to keep the children focused on what we are doing and helps make the transition flow more smoothly. The object is to communicate to the children a sense of belonging and of contemplation as we realize God is present here with us. A few friendly words of greeting, calling children by their names, will help communicate that Jesus does want them to be with him and he with them. Later chapters will provide more suggestions about creating a mood for prayer and praise.

5. First Reading

The readings are "the principal part of the Liturgy of the Word" (*General Instruction of the Roman Missal*, no. 40). Therefore, scripture readings should never be omitted. However, as the *Directory* recommends, "If three or even two readings on Sundays or weekdays can be understood by children only with difficulty, it is permissible to read two or only one of them, but the reading of the gospel should never be omitted" (Paragraph 42). This is why, for instance, the SUNDAY *Lectionary for Children* includes only one reading in addition to the gospel.

The first reading is usually taken from one of the books of the Old Testament. During Easter season, however, the reading comes from the *Acts of the Apostles*.

You may wish to have one of the children read, taking care that the child is adequately prepared.

Chapters 8 and 9 provide more background on adapting and proclaiming the word for children.

6. Response

The Response is usually taken from the *Book of Psalms*. They are sacred songs and we should sing them whenever possible. They convey the spirit and often explicitly embody the content of the reading, thereby enabling the children to remember and to carry God's word with them in their hearts. Chapter 11 develops and encourages the appropriate use of music.

The *Directory* makes this point: "Verses of psalms, carefully selected in accord with the understanding of children, or singing in the form of psalmody or the alleluia with a simple verse should be sung between the readings. The children should always have a part in this singing, but sometimes a reflective silence may be substituted for the singing" (Paragraph 46).

On occasion, the verses of the psalm may have to be read rather than sung. In this case, we should try to enhance the spirit of prayer with appropriate background music. Also, even if the verses are read, the children should sing the refrain.

7. Gospel Acclamation

This acclamation is a joyful greeting and acknowledgement of Christ's own presence here in the word. Therefore, we all stand when we sing the acclamation. Except during Lent, the acclamation includes the word *Alleluia*; the other words in the acclamation are taken from key sentences in the gospel of the day. Again, the words and music enable the children to remember and to carry God's word with them in their hearts.

8. Gospel

The celebration of the word leads up to this high point: the proclamation of the Good News. The gospel recounts the words and works of Jesus. While the *Directory* allows us to omit one or both of the other readings, "the Gospel reading, however, should never be omitted" (Paragraph 42).

We always stand during the reading of the gospel. If possible, the servers may stand by the reader with lighted candles. On occasion, you may want to incense around the book as well as around the children, symbolically conveying the presence of the Spirit of Christ in the word to be proclaimed and in the Word made flesh in the community.

9. Reflection on the Readings

When we reflect with children on the readings, we

must be sensitive to the presence of the Spirit in their lives. Children already have a spiritual life and relationship with God that Jesus himself used as the standard for entering the reign of God. Our reflections with children, therefore, should not be aimed at telling the children what we think they are supposed to hear. Rather, we should listen to what they have heard. This does not mean to suggest that we need not be prepared, that we need not reflect on the scriptures in light of our own lives. The point is one of attitude: let the children lead the way (see *Isaiah* 11:6). While our method of reflection may vary, our attitude is more one of listening and reflecting *together* on what God is saying to all of us.

Chapters 8 through 10 enlarge upon adapting the readings for children, proclaiming and nurturing the children's response to God's word.

10. Profession of Faith

The profession of faith or creed is a proclamation of what we believe in light of the word of God. The official creeds of the church (Nicene and Apostles') contain technical language and concepts foreign to most children. Chapter 12 provides suggestions on how to proclaim a simple creed that is integrated with the readings. Over time, all of the great statements of the community's faith can unfold and become part of the children's response in faith.

11. Prayer of the Faithful

The celebration of the word is that ritual event in which God speaks to us and we respond. It is God who takes the initiative. It is the Spirit who moves us to pray. So, in response to God's word, we offer the prayer of the community.

It is one form of response in the dialogue between God and the community of faithful. Because it is a response of the community, the prayer is best composed by the children themselves rather than by the leader alone. Chapter 12 deals more specif ically with ways we can nurture the children's prayerful response to God's word.

12. Return of Children to the Main Assembly

Timing the length of the children's celebration with that of the main assembly has to be worked out between the leaders and the priest presiding at the main assembly, making accommodations when one or the other needs more or less time.

Usually someone from the main assembly signals the leader of the children's celebration when the adults have begun their prayer of the faithful. If time is short, the children's leader may shorten the children's prayer of the faithful and conclude with the prayer of the day only.

The children rejoin the main assembly with less formality than when they processed out to their place of celebration. Their return usually happens during the collection and in time for the offertory procession. Experience has shown that the children's return is a joyous reunion with family members, often accompanied with hugs and smiles. Again, the movement of the children has the effect of refocusing the entire community on what it has been about and what is now about to happen: the Liturgy of the Eucharist.

———

Each of these components serves a particular purpose in the ritual celebration of God's presence in the word. They require careful planning and sensitivity to the needs of children. It is critical in this symbolic activity that the children enjoy a sense of belonging to the community. Such bonding grows out of sharing in the ownership of the community's rituals and out of the community's recognition and respect for the quality of spiritual life children bring to the community. For what other reason did Jesus admonish his disciples to "let the children come to me" (*Mark* 10:14)?

Discussion Questions

Note: The discussion questions at the end of each chapter reflect three parish situations: 1. For parishes that have not yet started celebrating the word with children. 2. For parishes that have just begun to celebrate the word with children. 3. For parishes that have been celebrating the word with children for several years. You can select questions that best complement your situation.

1. Reflect briefly with each other on the significance of each component in the structure of the Liturgy of the Word with children, starting with the Gathering Rites through to the return of the children to the main assembly.

2. The *Directory* makes the point that the Liturgy of the Word with children not be a new rite. What do you think is the significance of having the Liturgy of the Word with children follow the same ritual design of the Liturgy of the Word celebrated in the main assembly?

3. How can our parish benefit from celebrating the word with children?

4. What parts of the children's liturgy are in particular need of improvement in our parish?

5. What do we need to do to help our parish better understand the significance of celebrating the word with children?

6. How familiar are our parish leaders and particularly our children's liturgy team with the principles outlined in the *Directory for Masses With Children*?

7. What do we, as individuals and as a group, perceive to be the quality and character of the spiritual life of children? What is the relationship between the spiritual life of children and celebrating the word with children?

Chapter 2

WHY CELEBRATE THE WORD WITH CHILDREN?

Liturgy is ritual-making. Through ritual, people dramatize—make tangible—what they believe to be the hidden story of their lives. For Christians, their story is of life with Christ, the risen Lord, God with us.

Children are natural ritual-makers—and natural liturgists. So it is appropriate that they celebrate church liturgies and thereby come to develop a ritual literacy expressive of God's presence in their lives.

The word *liturgy* derives from the Greek *leitourgia* which is formed from two words meaning *people (laos)* and *work (ergon)*. In classical Greek, *leitourgia* meant any work undertaken on behalf of the people for the good of the community, such as education, prayer, defense or even the building of roads.

Over time, Christians gradually used the word to describe the public worship of the church. So, liturgy is the work of the people. Liturgies include all of the sacramental celebrations, the liturgy of the hours and rites of installation for liturgical ministries within the church, rites of religious profession and consecration, rites for the dying, the burial of the dead and for the dedication of a church. All of these public ritual actions either anticipate the eucharistic liturgy or extend from it. The eucharistic liturgy is the "summit towards which the activity of the Church is directed; at the same time it is the fount from which all her power flows" (*Constitution on the Sacred Liturgy*, no. 10).

Liturgy is the ritual prayer of the church. Rituals always involve relationships. The rituals in our lives help us develop and maintain identity within our families and communities. They provide safety and structure, especially for children, and shape who we are in relationship to one another.

Simple family rituals, such as birthday parties, bring generations together in a predictable pattern of telling stories, giving gifts, eating and singing together. Families celebrate birthday parties with children when they are still too young to understand or intentionally participate in them. Nevertheless, the ritual of gathering does provide children with a sense of belonging. Studies have indicated that children whose birthdays have not been celebrated often suffer a lack of identity and sense of self-worth.

As children grow, they gradually learn the words of the song, the significance of the cake, the joy of receiving gifts, and the knowledge of belonging to a family. When we share our rituals with others, we invite them to be part of our lives. Though barriers may exist, in ritual they come down, at least for a moment, as we dramatize the harmony that we believe is hidden in our lives.

Rituals draw children into the life of the church and give children their identity as Christians. Children gradually become initiated into the Catholic community by hearing its stories and sharing in its celebrations. The ritual action of the children's Liturgy of the Word establishes for children a sense of belonging to a group of believers who are known by their rituals. So do rituals give the adult community the opportunity to help children grow in faith as they look to the community for strength and guidance.

Adults, on the other hand, also benefit from children's sense of wonder, thirst for learning, and their desire for God. Through our liturgical rites we find strength in each other, we reinforce each other's faith and are challenged to live up to what we celebrate—to grow in Christ.

As with all ritual, liturgies follow familiar forms. The

eucharistic liturgy—the mass—follows a prescribed pattern: Introductory Rites, Liturgy of the Word, Liturgy of the Eucharist, and Concluding Rites. The liturgical assembly gathers as a community who has gone through the baptism ritual in order to enter the mystery of Christ and rise with him. Those who gather enjoy a kinship—they are related as members of the Body of Christ.

Through the Introductory Rites, the people prepare to listen to God's word and to celebrate the eucharist. During the Liturgy of the Word, the stories of God's action in human history are proclaimed and celebrated. As a child is formed by listening to and living with a parent, so a child listens to God's word and learns God's way.

Having heard the word proclaimed, we respond in song, praise and prayer, and we reflect upon how God is acting in our lives today. When we respond to God's spoken word, we are responding to Christ. "He (Christ) is present in his word, since it is he himself who speaks when the Holy Scriptures are read in church" (*Constitution on the Sacred Liturgy*, no. 7). The Liturgy of the Word—whether with adults or with children—is ritualized worship and prayer through which we make tangible God's presence with us today. This presence is further dramatized and fulfilled in the Liturgy of the Eucharist when, through bread and wine the word becomes flesh in us.

The Liturgy of the Word for children is not a new rite. It is the same rite, adapted for children, and designed as a way of *including* children in the Liturgy of the Word for the entire parish assembly.

Some would argue that separating children from the main assembly is a kind of dismissal, like that of catechumens before the Liturgy of the Eucharist. However, pastoral practice has shown that the Liturgy of the Word for children has given children a sense of belonging. The reason is simple: when they hear the scriptures in language they can understand, they feel included and are more able to share their responses with the family after the liturgy. The result is a sense of belonging to a community that once seemed for adults only.

Ideally, the celebration of the main assembly should incorporate everyone present, young and old. We need to work toward this ideal. An occasional parish succeeds. Most do not. Some try "family masses" with "children's homilies." Such practice, rather than weaving the children into the fabric of the parish family gathering, can risk using children as objects of display.

There are parish problems that affect the quality of our liturgies: cumbersomely large and impersonal parish gatherings, lack of homiletic skills of presiding celebrants, "turf conflicts" among parish leaders, hurried weekend Mass (i.e. parking lot) schedules, and general lack of ritual ownership on the part of parishioners. Whatever the parish circumstances, the children's Liturgy of the Word will not solve the larger problems but can lead toward liturgies respectful of all who gather. Certainly, if not carefully done, the Liturgy of the Word for children can be more harmful than helpful to children. With care, however, it can nurture in children a liturgical and biblical spirituality that is generally not available to them in the way that most main assemblies celebrate the Liturgy of the Word.

Moreover, as children who have richly celebrated the word become adults, they will bring to the assembly a greater appreciation for God's presence in the word. This does not mean to suggest that parishes can delay raising the quality of parish liturgies for adults as well as children. Such improvements need to continue, particularly in serving intergenerational needs. In the meantime, the children's Liturgy of the Word can nurture the spiritual life of your parish.

We need to keep in mind, however, that children's Liturgy of the Word is worship, a liturgical enterprise, not to be confused with "lectionary-based catechesis," "liturgical catechesis," or a substitute for systematic catechesis. Various documents make the point:

• The *Directory for Masses With Children*: "Even in the case of children, the liturgy itself always exerts its own proper didactic force" (Paragraph 12).

• The *National Catechetical Directory*: "Fruitful participation in catechesis calls for the spiritual enrichment that comes from liturgical participation" (No. 36).

• The *Constitution on the Sacred Liturgy*: Full and active participation in the liturgical celebrations of the church are the "primary and indispensable source from which the faithful are to derive the true Christian spirit" (No. 14).

Liturgies that are accessible to children, that complement their levels of understanding, and that are sensitive to the character and quality of their spiritual lives, are the life breath of any catechetical process. The *Directory* underscores the importance of liturgical formation, particularly the impact of God's word in liturgical celebrations:

"Various kinds of celebrations may also play a major role in the liturgical formation of children and in their preparation for the Church's liturgical life. By the very fact of celebration children easily come to appreciate some liturgical elements: for example, greetings, silence, and common praise (especially when this is sung in common). Such celebrations, however, should avoid having too didactic (instructive) a character. Depending on the capacity of the children, the word of God should have a greater and greater place in these celebrations" (Paragraphs 13, 14).

The *Directory* goes on to point out that every effort should be made to make the liturgy, specifically the Liturgy of the Word, understandable to children. "All the elements which will help to understand the readings should be given great consideration so that the children may make the biblical readings their own and may come more and more to appreciate the value of God's word. Among these elements are the introductory comments which may precede the readings and help the children to listen better and more fruitfully, either by explaining the context or by introducing the text itself" (Paragraph 47).

Elsewhere the *Directory* cautions, such introductory comments and explanations "should not be merely didactic" (Paragraph 23). At the risk of belaboring the point, the reason for liturgy is to worship God—not to teach lessons.

Moreover, the norm for holding the celebration of the word with children is year round, not just during the school year. Systematic catechesis may take place during summer Bible school or through the nine-month school year. However, worship is part of life, twelve months each year. So the liturgical year should be highlighted as part of children's lives for the entire twelve months, not just during the nine-month school year.

For the child, participation in liturgy takes place within a family context or in relationship with other adults in the community. Most children simply cannot get to mass without the assistance of family or community. The *Directory* focuses on the responsibility and formative influence of the family and community in this regard:

"A fully Christian life cannot be conceived without participation in the liturgical services in which the faithful, gathered into a single assembly, celebrate the paschal mystery . . . . By reason of the responsibility freely accepted at the baptism of their children, parents are bound in conscience to teach them gradually to pray. This they do by praying with them each day and by introducing them to prayers said privately. If children are prepared in this way, even from their early years, and do take part in the Mass with their family when they wish, they will easily begin to sing and to pray in the liturgical community; indeed they will have some kind of foretaste of the eucharistic mystery . . . . The Christian communities in which the individual families belong or in which the children live also have a responsibility toward children baptized in the Church. By giving witness to the Gospel, living fraternal charity, actively celebrating the mysteries of Christ, the Christian community is the best school of Christian and liturgical formation for the children who live in it" (Paragraphs 8, 10, 11).

Family and community shape the attitudes and values of children. So, too, are family and community responsible for bringing children into the Christian life through prayer, the word of God and the ritual celebrations of the church. Whether the children are unbaptized, baptized and completing their initiation, or fully initiated and growing in faith, they need the nourishment of God's word and the support of the community.

Children's Liturgy of the Word enables children to recognize the word of God as the foundation of all Christian communities. Children begin to make the scripture stories their own. They closely identify with persons in the Bible. The scriptures become the measure by which they judge their personal values, the quality and character of their lives—and of the lives of others in the Christian community. Through the ritual action of the assembly, children are gradually assimilated into the community's human values and, concurrently, into the biblical spirituality of the Christian community.

The *Directory* observes: "In this way, even if children already have some feeling for God and the things of God, they may also experience the human values which are found in the eucharistic celebration, depending upon their age and personal progress. These values are the activity of the community, exchange of greetings, capacity to listen and to seek and grant pardon, expression of gratitude, experience of symbolic actions, a meal of friendship and a festive celebration. Over and above what has been said already, all liturgical and eucharistic formation should be directed toward a greater and greater response to the Gospel in the daily life of the children" (Paragraphs 9, 15). That, ultimately, is the answer to the question, "Why celebrate the word with children?" To draw children into the life and work of Jesus so that God's word might take flesh in them, as it did in Jesus, giving glory to God every day in the way they share God's love—unconditionally.

Discussion Questions

1. Why celebrate the word with children?

2. What are some basic characteristics of ritual-making and of what significance is ritual in our lives? Of what significance are liturgical rites in the Christian initiation of children?

3. How can we enhance the quality of our ritual-making in our celebrations of the word with children?

4. List the differences between celebrating the Liturgy of the Word with children and giving children catechetical instruction.

5. Why is it important for children to hear the word proclaimed at the Liturgy of the Word in language they can understand?

6. How aware are we of the spiritual life of children? In what ways do we reflect the same respect for the spiritual life of children that Jesus expressed and exemplified?

Chapter 3

THE MINISTRY TEAM: WHO ARE THE MINISTERS OF THE WORD?

The number of persons on the ministry team and the role each member plays will vary with the size and circumstances of each parish. In smaller parishes, one person may "wear several hats." In other cases, several persons may "wear the same hat." In either case, the following roles represent areas of responsibility and of skill upon which successful celebrations of the word with children depend.

Before describing the specific roles, the point needs to be made that the team who ministers the word with children should not see itself as separate from the parish liturgical committee or team of liturgical ministers already serving the parish. In some parishes, the current lectors, musicians, hospitality, art and environment ministers may enlarge their service to include the children's Liturgy of the Word. If the current liturgy committee or team does not have the talent to work with children, then parishioners with those skills will need to be added to their number. It is important that the ministry with children be not only *perceived in theory* but also *organized in practice* as part of the ministry with the general parish assembly. Such coordination will reinforce the understanding that the Liturgy of the Word with children is an integral part of the Liturgy of the Word with adults.

Such organization complements the vision of the
Directory when it states: "The Christian communities to
which the individual families belong or in which the
children live also have a responsibility toward children
baptized in the Church. By giving witness to the Gospel,
living fraternal charity, actively celebrating the mysteries
of Christ, the Christian community is the best school of
Christian and liturgical formation for the children who live
in it" (Paragraph 11). It is always within the context of the
larger community that we celebrate the word with children.
Within this context the entire Christian community is part
of the ministry team that serves the children.

It may be worthwhile to recall that the word "ministry"
originates in the New Testament Greek term *diakonia*.
The word refers not only to those gifts we use to serve
those in need (*Romans* 12:7) but also to those gifts we use
to build up the body of Christ (*Ephesians* 4:12). In either
case, ministry clearly derives its power not from the
position we hold but from the service we give to others.
Jesus invites us to serve as he served, not for the sake of
one's prestige in the community, but for the sake of
building God's reign of kindness, compassion and mercy.
This is the task for which the Spirit has gifted the entire
assembly of baptized Christians—adults *and* children. So
the list of team members begins with the assembly
itself—adults and children—and includes such other
talented members as leader of the word, reader (or lector),
musician, art/environment minister, hospitality minister,
and coordinator.

The Assembly

Those gathered to celebrate the liturgy have the
primary and essential role of caring for one another. This
is what makes "liturgy" the "work of the people"—our
care for each other done for the glory of God. It is the
work we do in Jesus' name that we offer in praise of God
when we gather for the eucharistic celebration. Liturgy is
"the outstanding means whereby the faithful may express

in their lives and manifest to others the mystery of Christ
and the real nature of the true Church" (*Constitution on
the Liturgy*, no. 2). After Jesus Christ and the Holy
Spirit, the primary minister of every liturgy is the local
church assembled.

It was the custom of the earliest Christian communities
to proclaim the word in the assembly of believers. This is
the way early Christians—and we today—celebrate Christ's
presence: by gathering together in prayer, praise and
celebration in Jesus' name. We who gather minister to one
another through our attentive listening and responding to
the word proclaimed. Our response in song, prayer, gesture
and silent reflection celebrates the reality of Christ's
presence in our midst. Through our response we reflect
the level to which we have taken ownership of the ritual
and thereby manifest Christ's presence in the assembly.
We do not participate as spectators; rather, it is *we* who
perform the rite. We need to nurture this attitude and
understanding in children. We can do this in several ways:

• The first, obviously, is through the behavior of the
general assembly. Children learn by doing what they see
others do.

• Children understand gestures even before they
understand words. In both the parish assembly and
in the children's gathering, simple gestures—reaching
out to each other, raising one's hand in a sign of
blessing someone, hand-clapping—help nurture the
community's participation.

• When the leader of the word at the children's
gathering stands for the gospel, the movement and
posture communicates to children a sense of respect
and attentive listening.

• Parents can talk with their children—particularly
the very young—about the way they participate by
listening, singing, standing, sitting, kneeling together. If
parents do not start when their children are very young,
they will soon find it's too late. Even if the young child
cannot read or follow music, parents can give the child a

hymnal anyway because such "pretending" is, in the child's mind, full participation.

• Religious education and catechetical programs can help children learn to participate in liturgical celebrations by teaching them the significance of various gestures and movements, helping them learn a repertoire of songs and psalms, developing in those who are able the skill to proclaim the word. The liturgy itself is not the time or place for explicit instruction. As the *Directory* points out, "the liturgy itself always exerts its own proper didactic force. Yet within programs of catechetical, scholastic and parochial formation, the necessary importance should be given to catechesis on the Mass. This catechesis should be directed to the child's active, conscious, and authentic participation" (Paragraph 12).

The Leader

Titles for roles are sometimes problematic. What does one call the person who leads the children's reflections on God's word? Several possibilities have emerged, including "catechist," "children's lector," "minister of the word," and simply "leader."

The term "catechist" is accurate, if taken in its original meaning, or as one "anointed" to work with catechumens. However, those who gather to celebrate the word are not always "catechumens" in the strict sense. Also, the title "catechist" has become synonymous with religion teacher or religious educator—what one does in a classroom. The role and function of the person who celebrates the word with children is quite distinct from that of "catechist" "catechist" in the classroom teacher sense of the word.

Some prefer the title "children's lector." However, the role of "lector" in the general assembly is limited to reading the scriptures or "proclaiming the word." This person does not lead the community's reflections on the readings. In the context of the children's celebration of the word, the "children's lector" may or may not be the reader but does lead the reflections after the readings.

Others prefer the title "homilist." Some liturgists object to this title. They point out that, although the person who leads the reflections, in effect, does what the homilist does, the role of homilist is specifically limited to an ordained minister, a deacon or priest.

Still others prefer the title "minister of the word." This avoids the connotations of "catechist," "homilist" and "lector"; however, the title suggests that the role of "minister of the word" is something distinct from the role of members of the assembly—who are the primary ministers of the word to each other and in the world.

In an effort to avoid each of these possible misnomers, we have chosen here to use the title "leader" of the word. The leader may or may not be an ordained minister: "With the consent of the pastor or the rector of the church, one of the adults may speak to the children after the gospel, especially if the priest finds it difficult to adapt himself to the mentality of the children" (*Directory*, no. 24).

The leader of the word is part of the parish's larger team of liturgical ministers. This role requires of the person the ability not just to read the lectionary but to proclaim the word in a manner and style that complements the literary form of the text. This person should be able to engage the children in active listening through the dynamic use of language appropriate to the age and experience of children.

In other words, the leader needs to develop communication skills, especially in storytelling. This means employing graphic images, dramatic action, skillful inflections and sensitively timed silences. Clearly, the leader has reflected on the scriptures and internalized God's word so that the proclamation comes from deep personal faith and understanding.

The theological expression is true for leaders, "Grace builds on nature." While leaders need to develop their own gifts, they must also trust in the Spirit to work through them.

The leader is not a classroom teacher or babysitter, as significant as those services are in other settings. The

leader's primary task is to awaken in children a sense of
God's presence in the word proclaimed and in the Word
made flesh in their lives, to open the hearts of children to
God's word and nurture their response in prayer, praise
and Christian living.

What the leader does:
- Welcomes the children.
- Proclaims the Gospel.
- Leads the reflection on the scriptures.
- Leads the Profession of Faith.
- Introduces the Prayer of the Faithful.

Leaders can develop an alliance with children by calling
them by name. If this is not possible, eye contact, facial
expressions and animated gestures contribute to the quality
of the children's response to God's word. Leaders will
want to be sensitive to the changing mood of the children.

Equally important is the use of silence, not imposed
but won through the creation of moments of awe
and wonder.

Also, leaders need a good sense of humor, the ability
to be flexible and creative with the limitations of time
and setting.

Above all, leaders believe in the gospel and in its power
to transform lives. Leaders proclaim the word through
faith and then trust in the power of the Spirit to act in the
hearts of those who hear. Leaders consider their
continued growth in faith an integral part of their ministry
with children.

Parents, grandparents, godparents, sponsors, teachers,
single adults and others involved in the children's lives are
ideal candidates for this ministry. Children who see the
significant adults in their lives proclaim and reflect upon
God's word with them will be profoundly influenced by
their example. They will see Christians taking ownership
of church-related rituals, integrating liturgy with their
daily lives, and working at the building of a community
with Christian values.

The Musician

Musicians play a vital role in the celebration of the Word. How can there be a *celebration* without music? Liturgy, by nature, is musical and music is an integral part of every celebration. The musician's role is to enable the children to pray through song. Through song, children carry the word of God with them in their hearts.

Musicians should include cantors, song leaders, and instrumentalists if at all possible. Often such talent is not seen as essential to our celebrations with children. In many cases, parishes use no music at all simply because no one cares enough to make it happen. In other cases, parish leaders cannot uncover such talent in the community. Although there are strong musical traditions identified with various cultures—Hispanic, African-American, German, Polish, Irish, Oriental—the Catholic community still struggles to nurture its musical literacy. In the "American culture" we rarely gather just to sing together. We prefer to be entertained by professionals.

We need to work against this tendency in our efforts to celebrate the word with children. We do not need always to involve professional musicians, nor even people who have had professional training. We need to encourage anyone who can sing to learn a repertoire of songs to sing with children. The person can learn the music by listening to audio recordings.

"Singing is of great importance in all celebrations," the authors of the *Directory* point out, "but it is to be especially encouraged in every way for Masses celebrated with children, in view of their special affinity for music . . . . If possible the acclamations should be sung by the children rather than recited . . . ." (Paragraph 30).

The Reader

The reader may be an adult, a teenager, or an older child—just so the word is proclaimed clearly, respectfully, and with personal conviction. We need to keep in mind that this is no ordinary reading. We are proclaiming God's

living Word. The reader needs to be able to engage the
listeners' interest with a lively delivery and, if the
particular text calls for it, like a story.

The reader needs to practice, to be familiar with the
meaning of the words, not just their sounds. The Leader
will need to coach the young persons who read, help them
to handle the book of God's word with ritual grace and
respect, and help them to communicate the message of
the texts. For example, a good reader does not bury his
or her head in the book, but establishes eye contact with
the listeners. Together the reader and children share
the message.

The reader should be clearly seen by all of the
children and not hidden away among them. However,
readers should be comfortable in front of a group and avoid
mannerisms that call attention to themselves rather than
to the word proclaimed.

Art/Environment Ministers

The art/environment ministers offer assistance in
preparing the place for celebration. If the children gather
in a sacristy or a classroom or any other room used for
another purpose, the art/environment ministers are
responsible for arranging the space and re-shaping the
environment for worship. The talents required include
sensitivity to the use of liturgical symbols and effects that
communicate mood and spirit of the changing feasts and
seasons of the liturgical year. They will need to meet with
the leaders and musicians for prayer and planning.

They may need to work with the leader, for example, in
creating visual aids that complement the telling of a story
or that illustrate a particular reading. Also, they may
serve the musicians by printing the words of the response
and gospel acclamation on large sheets of paper so that the
children are better able to participate. (If the parish is
using visual aids such as those in the SUNDAY celebration
series which include the responses in large type, the
art/environment ministers might see to it that a different

family each week has an opportunity to paint and color the
scripture illustration for use the next Sunday).

Hospitality Ministers

Although everyone who works with children should
carry with them the spirit of hospitality and care, the
hospitality ministers are specifically responsible for
attending to the special needs that might arise, making
sure everyone is comfortable and feels welcome. They may
attend to the procession of the children, seeing that doors
are held open, and signal when the leader needs to end the
celebra tion with children in time with the ending of the
celebration of the word in the main assembly.

Hospitality ministers are also responsible for distributing
the adapted readings in leaflet form to families at the end
of mass. They should also be available to answer any
questions parents might have about the children's
celebration and how they might sustain the children's
response through the week at home.

The Coordinator

The Coordinator of the children's Liturgy of the Word
should be appointed even if the parish already has a
liturgy coordinator or liturgy committee. The coordinator
is responsible for recruiting team members, providing for
their training and development, scheduling the team
members for liturgies, guiding the planning and evaluation
processes, and meeting with the pastor, parish liturgy
committee, director of the RCIA and children's
catechumenate, parish staff and others as necessary to
share information and keep in communication. The
coordinator is one who displays the gifts of organization,
communication, patience, enthusiasm and good humor.

While the gifts of ministry are given to build the body
of Christ, it should be understood that those who serve are
accountable to the parish community. The ministry team
needs to work closely with all involved in parish liturgical
planning and activities. As with all parish leaders of

liturgical prayer and celebrations, the ministry team must be concerned about developing their competencies as well as their own spiritual growth.

The entire team needs to be trained in the skills of public prayer and worship. They must become familiar with symbolic language and the art of ritual-making, how body language conveys reverence, praise, celebration. They should be persons eager to improve themselves and the service they provide, open to new ideas and willing to receive criticism gracefully.

Above all, members of the ministry team must be or seek to become persons of prayer, grounded not so much in private personal piety but in the rich biblical and liturgical spirituality of the church. They should also be sensitive to the spirituality of children and approach children with the respect Jesus conveyed when he singled out children as those to whom the reign of God belongs.

Discussion Questions

1. Who are the various members of the ministry team, what does each contribute, and what talents are required of each?

2. What talents does our ministry team possess and what new talents are needed? How can we involve more adults in celebrating the word with children?

3. In what sense are the children themselves the primary ministers of the word?

4. How do our parish liturgies show respect for children and their full membership in the community by virtue of their baptism?

5. Explore a variety of plans to motivate parishioners to contribute their time and talent to celebrating the word with children. What are the most significant problems our parish faces in beginning and sustaining a quality celebration of the word with children?

Chapter 4

PLANNING, PREPARING. . . AND EVALUATING

We learn from both success and failure. The suggestions in this chapter are based on both. However, we learn even more when we evaluate our successes and failures in light of improving. So, if you've already been doing the Liturgy of the Word with children, we hope the suggestions that follow will complement what you have already learned, and that you find here an opportunity to re-evaluate your experience—and pick up a few ideas from what others have learned.

Starting the celebration of the word with children can be very simple. If your experience is like most other parishes, you will enjoy immediate satisfaction from the response of the children. While appealing to children, the celebration of the word also has appealed to parishioners so that finding volunteers has been generally easier than for other parish efforts. How does this happen? One parish, for example, recruited volunteers by having a "children's liturgy awareness Sunday." On this particular Sunday, parish leaders held a Liturgy of the Word for children at the main assembly so that the entire parish could enjoy the experience. When parishioners gathered for coffee and donuts after mass, thirty parents volunteered to help.

In another parish, the pastor takes time at least once a year to explain to the main assembly the significance of the children's Liturgy of the Word, and invites parents to go occasionally with their children to celebrate with them. Such support encourages the parents to take ownership of the ritual and not always turn their children over to the "experts."

While leading children's celebrations does take certain skills, we do a disservice to parents when we suggest to them that only a few are able to reflect with children on the scriptures or read or lead the children in song. These are all basic parenting skills—talking with children, reading to them, singing with them—performed in a ritual setting.

How many team members are needed?

Each team should include the leader, a musician (or song leader), and those others needed to help prepare the worship space and to "shepherd" the children in the procession from the main assembly. Ideally, the leader is two people—a husband and a wife or two single parents. The two can help each other through their reflections on the scriptures and in providing each other with a critique of the celebration.

Whether the leader is a married couple or two other parents, it is helpful to arrange for a back-up team in case members of the primary team cannot make it. This means that for each liturgy, two teams are prepared. This may seem redundant or a waste of time for those who prepare and then not lead. However, keep in mind that the "preparation" is not only for the benefit of the children but also for the spiritual benefit of the adults. It complements the adults' own participation in the liturgical life of the parish. That is one of the attractive features of this ministry—everyone is nourished by reflecting on God's word. What's more, having a back-up team takes the pressure off both married couples and single parents whose unanticipated family crises may cause last-minute cancellations.

The total number of required ministers will depend upon the number of weekend masses that include children's Liturgy of the Word and the number of groups of

children you may have at any one children's liturgy.
Ideally, one regular and one back-up team will be
scheduled for each liturgy.

Recruiting Volunteers
As we've already mentioned, the children's Liturgy of
the Word appeals to parishioners. It is less demanding
than taking responsibility for a religion class. Team
members need not schedule extra time into their week
aside from preparing for the liturgy they normally attend.
Team ministers need to make only two commitments:
- Agree to serve at the liturgy at which the children's
  celebration occurs.
- Agree to meet with the other members for planning
  the celebration and prayerfully reflecting on the
  scriptures.
Once an initial team is trained and established, new
volunteers can be invited to observe a children's liturgy
and attend a planning session. There is opportunity here
not just for the parents of the children who attend but for
everyone to serve—from young adults to grandparents.
Intergenerational teams are ideal.
When recruiting, you might want to establish a limit to
the length of service, perhaps for one liturgical season, or a
set number of Sundays, or one liturgical year. You'll want
to avoid thinking of a schedule that copies the nine-month
school model. The liturgical year is twelve months. Also,
you'll want to avoid switching leaders so often that you
lose continuity from Sunday to Sunday. One parish, for
example, has 13 leaders, each serves every 13th Sunday;
that may not place a burden on the leaders, but what is the
experience of the children? The *Directory* follows a
criteria that should apply in everything that we do:
whatever is to the spiritual advantage of the children.
While children enjoy variety, they also crave security in
continuity and order—which ritual provides.

Training Ministry Teams
When starting, the coordinator may gather together a

group of selected adults. These should include at least two leaders of the word, two musicians or song leaders, and several other talented people to assist with art and environment. Interested parents, parish leaders (members of the liturgical committee, parish council, school faculty, religious educators) may also participate in this pilot gathering in order to encourage communication and cooperation within the parish.

The time commitment for the initial team will be greater than for those who follow. When recruiting members for this initial group, emphasize the opportunity for personal growth in faith and the chance to lay the foundation for an important service in your parish. The initial group will meet as needed to understand the children's Liturgy of the Word and its significance in the Christian initiation of children, in the spiritual life of families and in the enrichment of the parish's liturgical life. Those who participate in this initial group should be able to communicate this understanding to others as questions arise.

Training can also include viewing video tapes on the children's Liturgy of the Word, attending workshops offered by diocesan or national facilitators, observing children's liturgies in nearby parishes and meeting with their teams.

Often the best training comes from observing others—learning from their mistakes as well as their skills. This is so when you add members to your initial parish team. Prospective team members can attend and participate in the children's Liturgy of the Word until they become familiar with the ritual and the children.

*A Suggested Plan for Beginning
the Children's Liturgy of the Word*

1. Introduce the concept to the pastor, parish staff, religious education committee, and liturgy committee.

2. Obtain approval to begin offering children's Liturgy of the Word, decide starting date, at what Sunday mass(es) you will have the children's Liturgy of the Word.

3. Recruit members of the initial ministry team.

4. Hold training sessions with the initial team at which you explore how to reflect with children on the scriptures, learn the music to responses and gospel acclamations, make yourselves familiar with several Sundays of readings and go through those with each other.

5. You might want to involve several selected families in a practice session. Have them evaluate your efforts. After this initial practice/evaluation session, you might want to announce to the parish a demonstration session for families who wish to come. This might be held briefly after one of the regularly scheduled Sunday masses or at a time convenient to families. Parents—and children—will have questions and concerns, such as about going to a separate place for the Liturgy of the Word. They will need to be reassured that the children's celebration is not mandatory but an opportunity for children to hear God's word in language they can understand, and so forth.

You might see the need in your parish to hold a more detailed demonstration session that takes more time than available between masses on Sunday. In this case, you may want to gather the families in church and proceed as you would at a Sunday liturgy. The children may process to their separate worship space for a brief celebration while the parents stay in the main church for discussion, or to view a video on the Liturgy of the Word. Or, the children may enter a procession but remain in the church for their celebration so that the parents can enjoy the experience with them. Any explanations given for the sake of the parents can be given for the children as well. Also, parents and children can visit the separate worship space together.

The object is not to make the children's Liturgy of the Word seem complicated. It isn't. However, it is important that everyone understand its significance and rationale, and that parents' and children's concerns be respected.

6. Provide announcements and explanations of children's Liturgy of the Word through the bulletin,

newsletter, at various parish organization meetings, from the pulpit.

7. Continue regularly to provide publicity and explanations based on the responses of the parents and children for at least the first year.

The Ministry Team's Planning Meetings

Planning for the next Sunday always begins with an evaluation of the previous Sunday's liturgy. Also, each celebration needs to be seen in the context of what went before and what comes after. Following the evaluation, therefore, the group reviews the readings for the next Sunday and the one after that. Then the group is ready to focus on the readings of the coming celebration.

Before meeting, each member might prepare in this way:

1. Relax, clear your mind and heart, and pray before reading the scriptures. Let God speak to you.

2. Read the scriptures several times. Those who will be proclaiming the word should practice reading aloud.

3. Reflect on God's word and its meaning in your life today.

4. Reflect upon the experiences of the children in light of the scripture reading. How might they hear God's word on this particular Sunday?

Suggested Structure for the Planning/Evaluation Meeting

1. Gathering prayer. This might be taken from the response of the previous Sunday liturgy.

2. Business/scheduling. Who will preside next week? Introduction/answering questions of new team members. Problems to solve.

3. Evaluate previous week's celebration(s). How can we improve: Procession? Proclamation of the word? Reflections with children? Music? Creed and Prayer of the Faithful? Environment?

4. Introduction of readings for next two weeks. Establish context of next Sunday's readings.

5. Reader for next Sunday proclaims the word for the

team. Share your reflections and insights with each other. How does God's word affect your life today? Share ideas on how to facilitate the children's reflections on the readings. How might the readings be understood by the children based on their experience?

6. How might the Creed and Prayer of the Faithful be integrated with the readings?

7. Final preparations. In light of your reflections on the readings, what preparations need to be made for next Sunday's celebration(s): Children involved as readers? Art to be prepared? Environment arranged? Special props? Does everyone know the music?

8. Concluding prayer. This might be taken from your reflections on next Sunday's readings.

9. "Break a leg." (Good luck.)

More About Evaluating

There's a limit to what we can learn from other people's experience and expertise. Then we're on our own. That's why it is so important to learn what we can from our own experience—by evaluating over and over what we are doing. While there are a variety of items to focus on in our evaluations—we've listed several below—there is one criteria by which we must judge everything we do: in what way are we serving, or failing to serve, the spiritual benefit of the children?

For your consideration:

• Personal growth of ministry team. Are the members aware of their growth in biblical and liturgical spirituality? Are they finding inner peace through their reflections on God's word? Are they growing in their commitment to serving the needs of children and families beyond celebrating with them? Is the ministry team perceived by the community as selfless in their service?

• Focus on the scriptures. Are the leaders' reflections with the children respectful of what God is saying and of the children's responses? Or do the leaders have a hidden agenda, a lesson they want to teach rather than letting

God's word be the center of everyone's reflections?

• Music. Do the adults sing enthusiastically with the children? Is singing and movement integrated with the proclamation of the word and the children's responses?

• Quiet. Are there appropriate times of silence? Are these moments natural—rather than imposed? Are they filled with a sense of God's presence, of wonder, of gratitude for God's goodness?

• Effectiveness of the environment. What works? What distracts the children? How well is the book of readings displayed? Is the lighting effective in creating the right mood?

• Are the children interested? How do they respond? Are there moments of awe? Delight? Humor?

• Behavior of the children. Are there "problem" children? What is the "problem?" How can negative behavior/attitude be made positive? Is our planning the "problem?"

• Attendance. Is the gathering intergenerational? Do parents occasionally participate? Is attendance regular? Is there a slump during the summer? If so, why? Is communication with the parish effective? Is the invitation to participate inclusive and welcoming? Do children with handicaps feel welcome without being singled out?

• Logistics. Do the children leave in procession gracefully? Is the children's worship space accessible to children and adults with handicaps? Is the duration of the children's liturgy smoothly coordinated with the main assembly? Is communication and coordination between the presiding priest and the children's liturgy leader clear and cooperative?

• Ownership of the rite. Are children and adults performing the ritual together? Or do some simply "attend" as spectators? Is everyone's identity recognized and respected?

This is not an exhaustive list but it should give you a start. You might want to draw up your own list of

evaluation criteria, keeping in mind what serves the
spiritual benefit of children.

Discussion Questions

1. What do we need to do to start the Liturgy of the
Word with children in our parish?

2. Who do we need to convince and what do we need to
do in order to communicate the value of celebrating the
word with children? How will we present the idea?

3. What other parts of the parish staff and organization
will we need to work with and involve? How will those
involved in catechetics overlap with those involved
with liturgy?

4. Who will we invite to form the initial team?

5. How will we finance the entire effort, including
preparation of the environment, purchase of materials for
leaders and parents?

6. What materials will we use? How much time do we
need to prepare for the initial celebration?

7. What methods are we using to evaluate our
celebrations? Are our methods thorough enough and our
evaluations frequent enough to improve our celebrations?

8. How do our parishioners relate to celebrating the
word with children—do they value the children's
celebration as a way of respecting the children's right to
full participation in the liturgy, or do they perceive of the
children's celebration as little more than a way of avoiding
having to deal with otherwise bored and restless children?

9. What is the response of children to the celebration
of the word? What is the response of parents?

Chapter 5

GATHERING AND INVITING THE CHILDREN TO CELEBRATE THE WORD

The point needs to be made from the start: the children are *invited* to celebrate the word. They are not *instructed* or *told* to do so, nor are they *dismissed* from the assembly. The children's celebration needs to be understood and managed in the ritual as an extension of the main assembly celebration, a concurrent and equally valid part of the same event. By so doing, adults do not experience the children's leaving as an interruption or disruption of the ceremony.

Some liturgists have expressed concern over having children leave the main assembly for a separate celebration of the word. The practice, some say, gives the children an experience of dismissal, of not being part of the parish community. Children who are baptized, they point out, have every right to remain with the community; those who are not baptized—the catechumens—may participate in the "dismissal of the catechumens" after the Liturgy of the Word and before the Liturgy of the Eucharist. Furthermore, the celebration for the parish community should accommodate and involve both the adults and the children.

The principle is right: children do belong to the community and their participation should be recognized and encouraged. We can put that principle to practice in a variety of creative ways and avoid faulty practice that gives children—and adults—a bad liturgical experience.

Not infrequently some parish leaders involve children in ways that do not respect children. They set children up to be "cute" or to perform for the adults. Similarly, the way children are invited to join in a liturgy of the word can be just as disrespectful of them when the style of invitation conveys to the children a sense of being inferior members of the community or that they are being dismissed from the really serious liturgical business of adults. So, how do we communicate the intent of the separate celebration, that is, to provide—in a way that is respectful of children—an opportunity for them to hear God's word in language they can understand?

First, the children need to be present in the main assembly for the Gathering Rite. Some parishes, though few, invite the children to leave the main assembly before the processional. Also, a few parishes have reported that children do not gather with their parents in the main assembly; instead, they go directly to their separate place and join the main assembly after the Liturgy of the Word. The reason given for these practices is often "to save time" or "to avoid disrupting the mass."

Neither of these practices, however, communicates either to children or adults that the children's Liturgy of the Word is an integral part of the parish assembly. Nor do these practices take advantage of the symbolic value of having children first gather with the larger assembly. Also, the community's act of sending the children to hear the word proclaimed in language they can understand is an exercise— and a celebration—of the larger community's ministry to the young. What's more, as one pastor pointed out, the children's procession to celebrate the word serves to focus the entire community's attention on its own responsibility to listen to God's word and respond wholeheartedly.

The Gathering Rite is intended to help form those assembled into a worshiping community, properly prepared and disposed to hear the word and celebrate the eucharist. The rite consists of the gathering song and procession, the Penitential Rite, Kyrie, Gloria and Opening Prayer according to the season of the liturgical year.

Children gather with the entire assembly for this rite. They come to mass, usually with their families, are seated with them and remain there until invited to process to their own worship space for the children's Liturgy of the Word.

At the opening processional, the leader of the children's liturgy—or one of the children—carries the children's lectionary and processes into the assembly with the other liturgical ministers and the presiding priest. While the lectionary for the adult assembly may be placed on the lectern, the children's lectionary may be placed on a stand in front of the altar or on the altar, according to local parish custom. When we carry the lectionary for children in with the adult lectionary during the opening processional, that gesture makes the point that the children's celebration of the word is an integral part of the grand gathering.

After the Gathering Rite, we need to take the time necessary to have the children leave the main assembly gracefully and with dignity. If we hurry, we suggest that the children are disruptive and the congregation is eager to "get rid of the kids." On the other hand, a procession of the children can heighten the community's sense of ritual-making.

Let's consider processions briefly. Processions are a natural part of ritual-making—not just the processions of entrance and leaving, but also processions that pay homage, in this case to God's presence in the word. Processions—otherwise known as parades to children—are a natural part of children's lives. Processions speak a language children understand. The entire community can enrich the experience by singing a processional song with the children. Processing and singing provides a sense of harmony and unity, of a people who share a common purpose, follow the same journey. Rather than disrupt, the children's leaving is part of the community's performance of the rite.

Before the children's procession begins, the presider, after the opening prayer, might say:

"Those who wish, may now come forward to join in the procession for the children's (or, for our younger members') celebration of the word."

Other options:

"Would those who wish to celebrate the Liturgy of the Word for children please gather now with the leaders of the word."

"May the children gather now who wish to celebrate the word together."

"We welcome now the children and those adults who wish to celebrate the word with them."

The community is standing as the children are coming forward. Meanwhile, the presider may remove the children's lectionary from the altar table or the book stand and hold it up for all to see. Two servers with candles may stand beside the presider.

While the children are gathering, the adult leader who will receive the children's lectionary from the presider also comes forward. If the children are too numerous for one group, they may gather at several places, each marked by a banner, candle-bearer, or a leader who may be holding a children's lectionary. Waiting until the children have gathered, the presider then commissions the leader by saying something like this:

"_____, receive the book of God's word. Proclaim it with our children—as we will proclaim it here—so that the Word of God will light their way and lead them with us all to life everlasting."

Other options:

"_____, with this book of God's word, I commission you in the name of our Lord, Jesus, to share with our children the story of God's unfailing love."

"_____, receive the book of God's word.
Proclaim it with our children that they may grow
secure in following Jesus, our Shepherd, all the days
of their lives."

"_____, in the name of our Lord, Jesus, I
commission you to share the bread of God's word
with our children that they may be fed with the food
of life everlasting."

If one of the children, representing the entire group,
comes forward to receive the children's lectionary from the
presider, the commissioning and blessing might go
something like this, addressed to the entire group:

"Children of God, receive the book of the word of
God. May it touch your hearts, inspire your
thoughts, and shine in everything you do."

Or:

"Children of God, receive the book of God's word.
Through the power of the Spirit, may it fill your
hearts with love and your lives with hope and joy."

Or:

"Children of God, receive the gift of God's word. May
your ears and hearts be open to celebrate and to
share the Good News with us all."

In some parishes, during this commissioning ritual, the
entire community raises its arms over the children in a
gesture of sharing in giving the blessing and commissioning.
In this case, after the book has been presented to the adult
leader or one of the children, the presider may say a
prayer, such as:

"Lord, Jesus, you said, 'Do not keep the children
from me . . . let them come to me.' Our children
gather to be with you today. Take them in your
arms. Guide them and all of us in your way now
and forever."

Community response:

"Amen."

Or:

"God of creation, open the ears and hearts of our
children—and of us all—so that we may hear your
word and give you glory now and forever."

Community response:

"Amen."

Or:

"O God, we long for the light of your word. Guide us
in your way of love and mercy now and forever."

Community response:

"Amen."

By ritualizing the invitation of the children in this way,
the entire community not only participates in but *performs*
the rite and is brought into focus on the proclamation of
the word not only for the children but also for the adults.
After the commissioning, the children follow the one who
is carrying the book to their separate place of celebration.
Some parishes have a cross-bearer lead the way, followed
by the person carrying the book, held high, and
accompanied by two servers with lighted candles.

As with all liturgical processions, the community
remains standing as the children leave. Also, during the
procession, the community joins with the children in
singing an appropriate psalm response or refrain. The
leaders of song who accompany the children should be
toward the front of the procession. If the leaders are last,
the children in front may not be able to carry the music by
themselves and, as they enter their celebration space, find
themselves so removed from the song leaders that they
stop singing.

When the music ministers position themselves toward
the front of the procession, then the children who follow

enter a room already filled with music. This arrangement helps to keep the children focused on the celebration and makes the transition from the main assembly to their separate place go more smoothly.

As the children enter their separate place, the person carrying the book continues to hold the book high, waiting for all to arrive. When all have gathered around and the song is concluded, in the reverent silence, the person holding the book carefully places the book on the stand facing the children for all to see. Another variation is to place the book on the stand when the children are just finishing the processional song. The point is to feature the gesture of displaying the book of God's word—the symbol of God's presence.

After the book has been enthroned, the leader welcomes the children and invites them to be seated. The role of the leader at this point is something of a host or hostess making guests into one's home feel welcome.

Everything that happens from the gathering in the main assembly to the gathering in the separate place influences the mood with which the children enter the celebration of God's presence in the word and prepare to hear God's word proclaimed.

After the celebration of the word, the children return to the main assembly with less formality. The presider may recognize the return of the children in an informal way, welcoming them to participate in the celebration of the eucharist. Because this return takes place during the preparation of the gifts, the assembly is seated so the children can readily find their parents.

Before closing this chapter, one question remains to be answered: Which children are invited to participate in this Liturgy of the Word? As we suggested earlier, anyone who wants to participate. There is, however, reason to distinguish some children from others.

Many children who participate will have been baptized, confirmed and have received first eucharist. Certain other children will have been baptized but will not have been

confirmed nor have received first eucharist. Still other
children of catechetical age who have not been baptized
constitute another group; they are catechumens and
remain with their catechists after the celebration of the
word and during the celebration of the eucharist.

The presider may wish to recognize these different
groups of children when inviting them to participate in the
Liturgy of the Word with children. Such a gesture, though
it may seem confusing to some, can serve to call the
community's attention to the initiation process about
which communities have been kept in the dark because of
our current sacramental-preparation practices.

The basic purpose of a special celebration of the
word for children is to acknowledge their full share in
the life of the community. With this understanding,
we are limited only by our creativity in the way we
incorporate the movements of children in the main
assembly's liturgical activity.

Discussion Questions

1. Reflect on the Gathering Rite from the children's
point of view. What are we doing that gives the children a
sense of belonging to the community? How can we
improve?

2. Does our style of inviting the children to participate
in the celebration of the word give our children a sense of
being *dismissed* rather than being part of the community?
What response have you heard from the children?

3. How does our Gathering Rite involve the children?
The adults?

4. How does our invitation to the children help focus
the adult community's attention on celebrating God's
presence in the word?

5. Reflect on the physical movements of the Gathering Rite and the children's procession. What do these movements signify to the children? To the adults?

6. How does the style of the presider affect the assembly for the Gathering Rite and invitation to the children? What is the presider's understanding of the invitation to the children and the ritual blessing/ commissioning of the leader?

Chapter 6

A COMMUNITY OF CHILDREN CELEBRATE GOD'S FAMILY STORY

The question often arises: How old are the children who gather for the Liturgy of the Word? Should 3- and 4-year-old children be included? Teenagers? We need to use our judgment with regard to what best serves the needs of individual children and families.

The *Directory* specifically addresses the needs of "children who have not yet entered the period of pre-adolescence" (Paragraph 6). Beyond this, the *Directory* does not specify a particular age group.

The *Directory* does, however, offer a basic guideline when celebrating the word with children: we need to be sensitive to the spiritual capacity of the children and strive to serve the spiritual advantage of the children. Specifically, the *Directory* states: "Depending on the capacity of the children, the word of God should have a greater and greater place in their celebrations. In fact, as the spiritual capacity of children develops, celebrations of the word of God in the strict sense should be held frequently, especially during Advent and Lent" (Paragraph 14). Also: "Everything depends upon the spiritual advantage which the reading can offer to children" (Paragraph 44).

Generally, the gathering for children's Liturgy of the Word includes children ages 5 or 6 years to 12 years, the ministry team and other adult parishioners or some parents invited to join the group in order to pray and celebrate with the children. Some children as young as 4 might also attend, though usually accompanied by an older brother or sister or a parent. Most very young children will usually stay with the parent or adult in the main assembly, although some parishes have organized a separate gathering of 3- to 5-year-old children. While these parishes usually consider this a "nursery" or "baby-sitting" service, such a gathering does provide an opportunity for an even more simplified celebration of the word than one would have for older children. That, however, is another subject for another book. While we do not want to disregard the authentic spiritual life of very young children, our concern here is with a celebration that generally complements children 5- to 12-years-old. Whether younger children want to attend should be left to the discretion of the parents and children.

On the high side of the age range, children older than 12 should be able to participate in the Liturgy of the Word with the main assembly. Of course, we need not prevent older children from attending if they so choose or if it is to their spiritual advantage. Generally, the young person knows and decides when to remain with the main assembly.

Even within the age range of 5 or 6 to 12 years, questions arise about how to accommodate such a widely varied group. Some suggest breaking the children into age groups, as one does for school. Liturgy for children, however, is not another form of classroom instruction. It is—as for adults—the ritual celebration of God's presence in the word and our response to God's word. In this context, our responses can be a source of enrichment for one another, regardless of our varied ages.

The role of the older children can be stressed as model, guide and helper for the younger ones, particularly as they approach adolescence and no longer want to be considered "children." What's more, older children can take a more active role as readers and leaders of song. If the group includes such children, the presider might want to use language in the invitation that is sensitive to their

self-perception. For example, inviting the "children and
young members of our community" to celebrate the word
avoids categorizing the 12-year-old children with those
several years younger.

It should be made clear, however, that leaders need to
help older children respect the responses of younger
children. Being older does not mean being superior. We
live in a society that does not value childhood. We rush
our children into "growing up." At our liturgies, we need
to value and respect the responses of young children.
They have a spirituality that Jesus himself used as the
standard for entering the reign of God. The young child's
sense of awe and wonder can be a source of inspiration for
older children—and adults. They are a source of grace for
the entire community.

If children's Liturgy of the Word is for children, why is
it desirable that a few adults who are not part of the
ministry team also attend? Order and supervision may
seem the obvious and practical reasons. However, the
Directory makes the most basic reason clear: "Since the
eucharist is always the action of the entire Church
community, the participation of at least some adults is
desirable. These should be present not as monitors but as
participants, praying with the children and helping them
to the extent necessary" (Paragraph 24). Although this
statement comes from that segment of the document that
focuses on masses with children in which only a few adults
participate, the same standard applies to the Liturgy of the
Word with children that is part of masses in which most
participants are adults.

Adults are models for children. In our liturgies for
children, adults of all ages, particularly parents and the
elderly, should be present as signs to children of those
ancestors from whom we inherit the story of God's
unfailing love—our faith. It is a custom in some Jewish
communities for the grandparent to pass the Torah to the
parent who, in turn, passes the Torah to the child, who
then proclaims the word of God. What a significant

statement that gesture would make, if a grandparent, then parent, would pass the book of readings to the child—or adult—who proclaims God's word at the children's liturgy.

We grow in faith by living in a community of faithful people. It is important for children, as for all Christians, to meet and interact with people outside their families who are faithful to God's word in everyday life and willing to stand up for what they believe. What's more, in the presence of an intergenerational community, children learn the relationship between their individual families and the larger community of the church, that their families' faith is part of a larger inheritance of faith. As children become acquainted with believers of all ages, they come to learn that the movement of God's Spirit continues throughout one's life and, indeed, from generation to generation. Adults, too, are nourished by the presence of the Spirit in the lives of children, revealed by their innocence, spontaneity and simple, trusting faith.

There is, however, a practical matter to consider: some children may be apprehensive about leaving their families for the children's liturgy. It should be made clear to families that participation is optional. If children feel insecure about attending alone, parents should feel free to participate with them until such apprehension is relieved.

On the other hand, some children might not want to participate because they like to do what adults do. They may regard children's Liturgy of the Word less interesting than the adult liturgy. Also, some parents may prefer to keep their children with them. Indeed, that may be to the spiritual benefit of those children. In the course of making that decision, parents may want to explore the benefits of the children's liturgy by attending a celebration with their children. The experience will help them to decide what best serves the spiritual advantage of their child. In such cases, the children often choose to participate regularly, while the parents participate occasionally. Most children will be eager to participate, when given the choice, and if they see the children's liturgy as important to the adults and a normal part of the Sunday parish liturgy.

Another practical question arises: what to do with large groups of children? Often parish leaders tend to divide the children into age or school grades rather than maintain mixed ages. It should be clear from what has been said about the significance of intergenerational gatherings that organizing children into a graded system for worship would not be to the spiritual advantage of the children. What's more, grouping children by age creates the sense that we will move through the ranks until we graduate into the "real" celebration in the main assembly.

When the need arises to divide a group of children—perhaps the number grows too large for the space available—then the group can be divided alphabetically by family name. This arrangement keeps children of the same family together and maintains groups with mixed ages.

Parish leaders who have large numbers of children and are starting a children's liturgy often ask, "What is the ideal number for a group?" While numbers are of influence, the size of a gathering is less important than the quality of the experience. Jesus seemed to manage as well on the hillside bank of the Sea of Galilee with 5,000 followers as he did with just two at Emmaus. Obviously, a group of 30 or fewer offers more opportunity, than does a larger gathering, for individual children to express their response to God's word.

There is no one solution to every parish's, nor every child's, needs. Parents and parish leaders must make the judgment as to what arrangement best serves the spiritual advantage of the children. Ultimately, whether the gathering is large or small, in a sacristy or special children's chapel, the quality of the celebration depends largely upon the extent to which those present feel responsible for the ritual, *performers* in the drama of God's personal, incomprehensible and unfailing love for us.

Adults who are present at the children's liturgy carry a special responsibility—not as monitors but as model celebrants. Their attitude, their gestures and response to the sacred influence the spirituality of impressionable children. Children learn to believe through experiences shared with believers. They mature by seeing themselves in relation to others who are older and younger than they. The child is socialized into the community of faithful by others—adults and other children—who together interpret the meaning of events in their daily lives in light of God's personal involvement and self-revelation in human experience. How blessed we are with such good news to celebrate!

Discussion Questions

1. Share ideas on using the talents of older as well as the young children in the Liturgy of the Word.

2. What is our understanding of the reason for an intergenerational gathering for the children's liturgy, involving mixed ages of children and some adults? How do we involve adults, particularly elderly members of the parish, in the children's liturgy without taking away from the focus of the celebration on the needs of the children?

3. How can the leaders guide the reflections on the readings so that they are meaningful to the entire age range of children in our gathering?

4. Discuss the logistics of the number of children attending the children's Liturgy of the Word. How are we dealing with the numbers? Is our way of dividing the group serving the spiritual needs of the children? Are we giving the children the impression that they are being placed into age groupings, as in school? What are our plans should the number increase? Decrease?

Chapter 7

CREATING A SPACE
WHERE CHILDREN
CAN CELEBRATE THE WORD

One of the most frequent obstacles parishes face when wanting to arrange for a Liturgy of the Word with children is finding a place in which to gather. Some parishes have space in buildings removed from the main church. Processing children through a parking lot or across a street not only takes time, but tests the capacity of the children to stay in focus on the liturgy. Nevertheless, some parishes do just that—successfully!

Other parishes have only cafeterias, classrooms, libraries, sacristies or even hallways and stairwells. Chances are slim that your parish building design included the eventuality of celebrating the word with children. We face the problem, again, of having to function in buildings that fixed people into patterns of behavior that no longer serve the needs of the community. We may shape our buildings but eventually our buildings shape us. However, while our building designs can present real obstacles to serving the community's changing needs, we face even greater barriers when we let our buildings limit our vision and cripple our imagination.

In a sense, you can celebrate the word with children anywhere—parking lot or park, playground or parish house, convent parlor or cathedral palace. "Wherever two are gathered in my name," Jesus tells us, "I am with them" (*Matthew* 18:20). God's word and God's people, these are the basic ingredients. Beyond these, we can influence our environment to heighten the experience of God's presence when we gather to listen and respond.

As we explore ways of shaping new or re-shaping old places for worship, we will want to keep in mind that ultimately the attitude and manner of the leaders and children are the primary media of God's presence in the word proclaimed and the Word made flesh in us. Everything else serves that presence of God—in people. Space, place, or things no matter how sacred do not substitute for God's presence in people. "You are the temple of God," Paul tells us and passionately adds: "If anyone destroys God's temple, God will destroy that person; for the temple of God, which you are, is holy" (*1 Corinthians* 3:16-17).

The *Directory* also emphasizes the point: we are to do what is necessary to serve the spiritual benefit of the children. With this in mind, we'll go through a list of items that can influence the quality of the celebration.

Displaying the Book of God's Word

Next to the children, this is the central symbol of God's presence in the liturgy of the word. First of all, the book itself should be handsomely bound and decorated—a book that speaks in its appearance of celebration. The stand upon which the book rests should be attractive and feature the book rather than call attention to itself. If you do not have a bookstand, you may want to cover a small table or a child's desk with a cloth draped to the floor. The color of the cloth might be chosen to complement the liturgical season. Place the book on top and prop it up, perhaps with a small pillow under the cloth covering, so that the children can see the book.

If you use a lectern or a music stand covered with a cloth, display the book facing the children rather than the reader. When time comes to read from the book, the reader reverently lifts the book from the stand and holds it in hand while reading. The reader need not read from

behind the stand unless you wish to design a stand that
has a place in front on which to display the book and a
place behind on which to rest the book while reading.

The height of the lectern or stand should be lower
than the normal adult lectern, to complement the size of
the children. Sometimes parishes use lecterns designed
for adults—often left-over furnishings—which are less
than adequate for children. Often these lecterns are so
large they call more attention to themselves and hide the
proclaimer of the word as well as the book of God's
word itself.

On either side of the displayed book, you might want to
place lighted candles. These candles might be the same as
those carried in the procession and placed there with the
book when the children gather around.

Some readers may feel that these comments are
addressing the obvious. However, I have visited parishes
that have made no accommodation for the book. In one
instance, when the children arrived in the room, the
leader took the book from the child who carried it in the
procession, and when she sat down on the carpet (the
children sat in small chairs), she simply plopped the book
on the floor beside her as you would a magazine you had
just finished reading.

There are less formal ways of celebrating the Liturgy of
the Word with children than might be suggested by the
way in which we are describing the display of the book
with candles. However, we need to be aware of the
symbolic value of everything that happens when we gather
to make ritual. The way we move and handle sacred
objects reveal an inner disposition and communicates to
the children an attitude of reverence—or lack of it—for
what eye cannot see and ear cannot hear. The book is the
symbol of our inheritance of faith, of God's self-revelation
through human history, of God's uncompromising
covenant of care for us here and now. While the book is
paper and ink, it also represents a treasure too sacred to
handle with casual abandon on a ritual occasion.

Transforming Settings

Many parishes have to make do with the space available while others have been able to refinish and refurbish church basements or former classrooms into full-time children's chapels. In one parish, for instance, a group of parents took it upon themselves to finish off part of the basement of the church and furnish it expressly for the children's Liturgy of the Word.

Another parish already had a "weekday chapel" that parish leaders used for the Sunday children's liturgy. In this case, they made duplicate copies of the seasonal banners in the main assembly in order to convey to the children that their celebration in the chapel is the same as the one in the main church.

But what do you do if you have only a sacristy or classroom to use?

Sacristies are usually smaller than classrooms. Three or four strategically placed banners—not necessarily with designs or words on them—can suggest an atmosphere of celebration. They need not be large—perhaps five feet tall and three feet wide, made of plain yardage. Their color can change to complement the changing liturgical seasons. A three-panel space-arranger or room-divider can serve as a backdrop for the book of readings and place of proclamation of the word.

Similar kinds of banners can serve in creating a celebration setting in a classroom. In this case, the desks should be moved out of the way. Place the seasonal banners or space-arrangers in such a manner as to suggest an enclosure in which the children gather. The children should not use the desks; that would then risk making the experience for them overpoweringly one of being schooled.

When you push the desks away to clear a space, the children can sit together on the floor. If the room is not carpeted for seating comfort, arrange with a local dealer to get carpet samples or a remnant large enough to fill the space.

You may also want to consider making or purchasing

space-arrangers on which to display artwork by the
children or posters illustrating the scripture readings.
(See *Bibliography & Resources* for source of posters.)
Such posters and graphics help shape a liturgical setting
in keeping with the recommendations of the *Directory*:
"The use of pictures prepared by the children themselves
may be useful, for example, to illustrate a homily, to give
a visual dimension to the intentions of the general
intercessions, or to inspire reflection" (Paragraph 36).

Ideally, the children, or a different family each week,
paint it or color the weekly Sunday scripture posters. As
each season unfolds, the children become surrounded with
the unfolding, illustrated story of God's unfailing love.
Also, such involvement enables the children and families
to take ownership of the ritual. The Liturgy of the Word is
not a celebration created by a few adults for children to
attend; rather, it is a celebration created by the children
themselves, responding to God's word, under the guidance
of adults sensitive to the spiritual needs of children.

Lighting

An often-overlooked influence upon creating a
prayerful, liturgical setting is lighting. If you have to
gather in a classroom, instead of using the overhead
lighting, use one or two lamps placed in the area of
celebration that you cleared of desks. You may even pull
the window shades to subdue the bright light coming
through the windows.

We can take a lesson from hard-sell lighting of
department stores and, in contrast, the conversation
lighting of restaurants. Department stores are brightly
lighted in order to heighten the stimulating effect of the
products for sale. Restaurants are more dimly lighted,
often with lamps or candles on each table, in order to
reduce stimulation and create a quieting, relaxing
atmosphere. (Fast-food restaurants are usually brightly
lighted to stimulate fast sales to fast-paced patrons.)

As a rule of thumb, overhead, ceiling light is noisy and

stimulates activity. Indirect lighting is more calming and promotes quiet. A dimly lit room complements reflection.

A small spotlight on the book of readings can heighten the symbolic value of the book as the symbol of God's presence. Inexpensive, small spotlights with portable stands are available at your local photographic supply or video camera store. If the room is dimly lit, the light of candles by the book will heighten the inner sense of the sacred.

Arrangements and types of seating

When you are working with a group of children whose ages range from 5 years old to 11 or 12 years old as well as several adults, seating can be a problem. Should you provide chairs for the older children and adults or have them all sit with the younger children on a carpet? Or should you provide a variety of seating to accommodate the varying sizes of the children gathered?

Some parishes separate the younger children from the older ones. In such cases, usually the younger children sit on a carpeted floor and the older children use chairs.

When chairs are not available for everyone, some of the children—particularly the older ones—may perceive sitting in a chair as a symbol of being grown up, so they rush to get to those seats before the younger children.

Leaders may consider this to be a discipline problem; however, such a response by the children can also be interpreted as an illustration of their sensitivity to symbol and ritual. You may want to try different seating arrangements in the course of a year rather than arbitrarily decide how to arrange the children's seating. For example, if you regularly use chairs, you might sometimes want to remove them when they interfere with involving the children in body movements.

When you do have seats, arrange them in a circle or semi-circle, which is more symbolic of a community gathered to share its reflections, rather than straight rows of chairs, symbolic of a group gathered to hear an expert lecture.

Often when we create environments for worship, we overlook the most significant and strongest influence on the environment: the people who gather there. We are each other's environment. Our arrangement and our movements influence the quality of the ritual experience. We need to be sensitive to what the children are saying by the way they arrange themselves. How do the older children treat the younger ones? Do they look out for them or do they look out only for themselves? How can we encourage the children to respect and care for each other? The environment we, the leaders, create by our behavior, serves as a model for the children to follow.

Because people are the most significant expression of God's presence in our liturgical gatherings, we encourage a few adults, particularly older adults, to celebrate with the children. They are not there to police but to participate. The symbolic value of having elderly present with children communicates to children a holistic expression of community and, again, serve as models for the children to emulate as they grow up. If we do not provide such inter-generational learning, children will have only each other's immaturity as models for growth. The people who gather with the children play a vital part in shaping an environment that nurtures the spiritual growth of our children.

One parish leader invited an elderly parishioner to celebrate with the children. She was delighted by the experience, not to mention being complimented by the respect shown her value to the community. So, too, parents should feel free to participate on occasion at the children's Liturgy of the Word. More often than not, adults who have attended the children's liturgy attest: "I got as much out of that as the kids did." Such participation significantly enriches the liturgical environment in which both adults and children grow in the awareness of God's Word made flesh in the very young and the very old.

Discussion Questions

1. What are some basic characteristics of a good worship space for the children's Liturgy of the Word? How does the environment affect worship?

2. What are our options for a worship space for children's Liturgy of the Word? What are the obstacles to the space available? What are the advantages?

3. How can we improve the worship space we use? How well does it work?

4. How do we display the book of God's word? Does it communicate to the children a sense of God's presence?

5. What "things" are in our worship space? What symbolic value do they have for the children?

6. What effect does the lighting in our worship space have on the mood of the children? Is it conducive to reflective celebration?

7. How does our seating arrangement affect the children? What does the arrangement say to children about our relationship to each other in the presence of God?

8. The chapter makes the point that those who assemble are a significant part of the environment. How does the behavior of the adults who participate with the children affect the children's attitudes and sense of worship? How does the behavior of the older and younger children affect each other?

Chapter 8

ADAPTING THE READINGS FOR CHILDREN

"What was from the beginning,
   what we have heard,
   what we have seen with our eyes,
   what we looked upon
   and touched with our hands
   concerns the Word of life—
   for the life was made visible;
   we have seen it and testify to it
   and proclaim to you the eternal life
   that was with the Father and was made visible to us—
   what we have seen and hear we proclaim now to you,
   so that you too may have communion with us;
   for our communion is with the Father
   and with his Son, Jesus Christ.
   We are writing this so that our joy may be complete."
                                          (*1 John* 1:1-5)

The joy of the resurrection filled the first disciples. The desire to proclaim the Good News consumed them. To this day, the church continues to proclaim the same Good News of God's faithful and unconditional love. This proclamation takes place especially in the scripture readings at the Liturgy of the Word. The Second Vatican Council emphasized the teaching that God is truly present to us in the Sacred Scriptures. This word reveals God's saving love and nourishes our faith on our journey through life. For this reason, the church teaches that all Christians should have easy access to Sacred Scripture and encouraged scholars to translate and prepare versions of the scriptures that more people could read and understand.

The church is also concerned with making the scriptures available and understandable to children who, as full members of God's family, have their rightful place in the Christian community. Jesus made a special point of welcoming children. In his great love for them, he put his arms around them and blessed them. These children, as Jesus made clear to those who thought they were a bother to him, have the right to hear God's word. God wants them to hear it. However, we are all aware that children have difficulty understanding scriptures written in adult language beyond the capacity of children.

Happily, the Congregation for Divine Worship recognized this problem and provided a means for solving it. The *Directory for Masses With Children*, issued on November 1, 1973, opens the way for fulfilling the desire of parents, catechists, liturgists and priests to make the word of God understandable to children. This challenging document calls us to use "words and signs" in our liturgies which are "sufficiently adapted to the capacity of children" (Paragraph 2). Especially with regard to the scripture readings, the *Directory* encourages us to make selections and adaptations of texts guided primarily by the "spiritual advantage which the readings can offer children" (Paragraph 44).

Everyone who ministers to children, especially parents who long to share their faith with their own children, are keenly aware of the need for such adaptation. However, what criteria are we to follow in choosing a lectionary for children or in further adapting children's lectionaries to accommodate the needs of a particular child or group of children we are serving? Here are four basic principles to use as a guide, based upon the *Directory for Masses With Children.*

1. Retain the Sunday Readings of the Liturgical Year.

The church has selected readings from both the Hebrew and Christian scriptures, including nearly every book in the Bible, to be read over the course of three years. These readings put us in touch with God's action in human experience throughout the ages, and, through these readings, God calls us to respond in our own time.

In the Liturgy of the Word, children, too, receive God's wonderful revelation through the scriptures, and God invites them to respond in their daily lives. In this way, the children have the opportunity to experience the mystery of God's love for them as that grand story unfolds during the liturgical year. So that children, united with their families and the rest of the Christian community, may live the life of Christ through the liturgical year, it is important that the order of the scripture readings in the Liturgy of the Word with children be the same as the readings for adults. Some readings, however, are particularly problematic for children. In those instances, as the *Directory* recommends, an alternative reading may replace it.

"If all the readings assigned to the day seem to be unsuited to the capacity of the children, it is permissible to choose readings or a reading either from the Lectionary for Mass or directly from the Bible, taking into account the liturgical seasons" (Paragraph 43).

An example might help clarify this situation. The first Sunday of Advent in all three years calls us to prepare for the Second Coming of Christ. The gospels use many images to illustrate this event.

Year A, taken from the Gospel of Matthew, presents our need to be ready through the story of a thief breaking into a house. The evangelist tells us what we already know: if the owners knew the time the thief was going to break in, they would certainly stay home and be on the alert. The author draws the conclusion for us: We do not know when the Lord will return, so we must always be ready. It's a simple analogy that children can readily understand.

Year B gives us Mark's image of the Second Coming.

He tells the story of a home owner who, before leaving for a journey, parcels out the household duties to the servants and tells one servant "to guard the door very carefully." Again, the author draws the conclusion: We do not know when the owner (Lord) will return, so we must be awake and ready. Children will easily understand Mark's analogy, as they do Matthew's.

Year C, taken from the Gospel of Luke, presents a problem. Luke describes the need to be ready for the Second Coming in graphic, apocalyptic imagery. We hear that "nations will be in anguish, distraught at the roaring of the sea," "men will die of fright," "the powers in heaven will be shaken." We must be on guard "lest your spirits become bloated with indulgences" for this day will come upon us "like a trap." Even with adaptation, these images frighten children. The idea of being ready, and not to be afraid, would be lost on children. In instances such as this, it is our judgment not to use Luke, but substitute either Matthew or Mark in Year C.

The point needs to be emphasized: readings are not to be changed or dropped arbitrarily. The *Directory* standard is quite clear: "If three or even two readings on Sundays or weekdays can be understood by children only with difficulty, it is permissible to read two or only one of them, but the reading of the gospel should never be omitted" (Paragraph 42). Based upon this guideline, the SUNDAY *Lectionary for Children*, for example, always includes the gospel and one of the other two readings.

2. Remain Faithful to the Meaning of the Text.

When choosing a lectionary or when further adapting a text for children, it is important to remain true to the meaning of the text. This requires attending to two basic matters of concern.

First, the text may not be a paraphrase. *After you have proclaimed the word*, it may be appropriate to use a modern-day story with the same theme as the text when reflecting on the word with children. However, *it is not appropriate* to "modernize" images in the text or use a modern story in place of the sacred text when adapting the reading for proclamation. The *Directory* makes the point this way, quoting from the "General Instruction of the Roman Missal": "In the biblical texts 'God speaks to his people . . . and Christ himself is present through his word in the assembly of the faithful.' Paraphrases of scripture should therefore be avoided. On the other hand, the use of translations which may already exist for the catechesis of children and which are accepted by the competent authority is recommended" (Paragraph 45). Based upon this recommendation, for example, the Canadian Conference of Catholic Bishops endorsed the SUNDAY *Lectionary* for use in liturgies with children.

Second, the beautiful and varied literary styles of the sacred writings should be retained. The Bible contains prose, poetry, parables, stories, and even outrageous hyperbole. Often the message relies upon the style of writing and the rich images. For example, the 24th Sunday of Ordinary Time (Year C) tells us about a woman who turns on every light in the house and sweeps every room to find a single, lost coin. Then, after finding this single coin, she plans a party with her friends and neighbors—presumably at far greater expense than the coin would cover. Children are not likely to take this story literally or stumble over the obvious exaggeration of the story. Nor will they miss the conclusion: Everyone in heaven rejoices over one person who stops sinning and comes back to God. Some may want to make the story "relevant" for children and "fix" what seems so outrageous in the story. By so doing, we miss the point: *God's love for each of us is outrageous.*

Since Christ himself is present in the word, we can rest assured he will speak to the children (and adults) on some appropriate level. Although we want children to understand the word, we know that every child will not understand immediately. Nevertheless, like seed, the word will take root and grow as the children hear God speak to them year after year and reflect upon what they hear God saying to them.

3. Use Language That is Intelligible to Children.

The *Directory* emphasizes again and again the need to proclaim the word of God in language children can readily understand and apply to their daily lives. The word of God is the source of nourishment in our lives as disciples of Jesus. Children, too, are called to follow Jesus. They need—and want—to hear Jesus speak to them.

More often than not, the message is as relevant and fitting for children as it is for adults. However, children often fail to hear the message simply because it is couched in language beyond their comprehension. When we look at a reading, we might ask ourselves, "How would Jesus have said this same thing to children?" How can we say this to children while remaining true to the meaning and style of the passage? We must make every effort to present the readings in simple, direct language. Often the meaning of an entire passage will come clear to children when we reduce multi-syllabic words to simpler vocabulary. Or we can clarify the message by rearranging the order of words in a sentence, or simplifying sentences. When sentences are unusually long or contain several clauses, they can be separated into shorter, more direct sentences. For example, consider the first reading for the 5th Sunday in Ordinary Time (Year A), from the prophet Isaiah:

"Thus says the Lord:

'Share your bread with the hungry,
and shelter the homeless poor,
clothe the man you see to be naked
and turn not from your own kin.
Then will your light shine like the dawn
and your wound be quickly healed over.

'Your integrity will go before you
and the glory of the Lord behind you.
Cry, and the Lord will answer;
call, and he will say, "I am here.""

'If you do away with the yoke,
the clenched fist, the wicked word,
if you give your bread to the hungry,
and relief to the oppressed,
your light will rise in the darkness,
and your shadows become like noon.' "
(Isaiah 58: 7-10)

A brief scanning of this passage illustrates how many
words and phrases are beyond the comprehension of
children. Nevertheless, the meaning of the passage is not
beyond them. Here is an adaptation of the same text as it
appears in the SUNDAY Lectionary:

"Our God says,

'Share your bread with those who are hungry.
And when you see people who have no home,
give them a place to live.
Give clothes to anyone who needs them
and be kind to your own family.
Then you will be like the morning light
that comes after the darkness of night,
and your sins will be forgiven.

'You will call upon God to help you,
and God will say, "Here I am!"

'Don't hurt people by lying about them
or by saying unkind things about them.
Give bread to the hungry
and help those who suffer.
When you do these things,
your gloom will be changed to joy,
and you will shine with the brightness of God's light.' "

This adaptation makes the passage understandable to
children while retaining the flavor of the language and
meaning of the original text.

4. Use Language That is Inclusive of All God's People.
Since the renewal of the liturgy, which made possible

the use of the vernacular, the Christian community has become more aware of the language used in liturgical celebrations, especially the eucharist. While this language has been almost exclusively masculine, many now recognize that whatever the origins of this practice, both historical and grammatical, the use of exclusive language does not accurately represent the meaning of the Sacred Scriptures nor what the church should be. Revisions of liturgical texts and translations of the Bible, therefore, should avoid language that implicitly or explicitly excludes women, for example, or that subtly conveys prejudicial attitudes toward any individual or group.

In its document issued November 15, 1990, *Criteria for the Evaluation of Inclusive Language Translations of Scriptural Texts Proposed for Liturgical Use*, the National Conference of Catholic Bishops recognizes and wishes to respond to "this complex and sensitive issue of language." In presenting guidelines and principles for inclusive language in the liturgy, the bishops write: "The language of biblical texts for liturgical use should be suitably and faithfully adapted for proclamation and should facilitate the full, conscious, and active participation of all members of the Church, women and men, in worship."

The bishops suggest some possible adaptations which would aid in this active participation of all God's people. For example, masculine references formerly understood as generic, such as men, sons, brothers, forefathers and so forth, are no longer understood as such and "should not be used when the reference is meant to be generic." The gospel for the 19th Sunday in Ordinary Time, Year B, provides an example. The line, "If anyone eats this bread he shall live forever," might be rendered simply, "Anyone who eats this bread will live forever."

The bishops, furthermore, suggest the use of the second or third person plural where the sense of the original text is universal. For example, the gospel of the 22nd Sunday in Ordinary Time, Year A, reads: "If a man wishes to come after me . . . ." Because this sentence is preceded by "Jesus then said to his disciples," we might adapt as follows: "If you want to come after me . . . ."

Throughout the document, the bishops clearly place emphasis on rendering texts inclusive without altering the meaning of the sacred writing.

Children particularly need to hear language that is inclusive because they readily relate more to concrete terms rather than to abstract concepts. The use of exclusively masculine or feminine language at liturgical celebrations may solidify for them a limited image of God, God's people and ministry in the church. Nuances in language imperceptibly plant wholesome or prejudicial attitudes in children. The readings in liturgical celebrations proclaim God's saving word for all people, a message equally important for children as well as adults to hear and understand.

Equally important, any adaptation for children that reflects sensitivity to inclusive language must read smoothly. The choice of language, in such cases, does not call attention to itself and, thereby, distract from the meaning or deviate from the style of the text. In applying this fourth principle for adaptation, we return to the over-riding guideline of the *Directory for Masses with Children*, that all of our efforts must be guided by the "spiritual advantage which the readings can offer children" (Paragraph 44).

Discussion Questions

1. Reflect on the significance of each of the principles described in this chapter:
   a. Retain the Sunday readings of the Liturgical Year.
   b. Remain faithful to the meaning of the text.
   c. Use language that is intelligible to children.
   d. Use language that is inclusive of all God's people.

2. What do we do to assure ourselves that we are following these principles? Are these principles used in our evaluation process?

3. What process and principles did we follow (or will we follow) in selection a children's lectionary?

4. When we find that we may need to further adapt the readings for our particular gathering of children, how do we critique each other so that we are true to the principles of adaptation?

5. How careful are we in our reflections with the children to remain true to the meaning of the text? When the children hear something that we think is not apparently related to the meaning of the text, how do we respect the child's understanding and response to the text? Are we sensitive to the principle that our purpose is not to teach content but to celebrate God's presence in the word?

6. How important to us is the use of inclusive language? Are we sensitive to the use of inclusive language in our reflections with the children?

Chapter 9

PROCLAIMING THE WORD AND NURTURING THE CHILDREN'S RESPONSE

Imagine walking with Jesus, listening to his teaching, witnessing his miracles—then, having everything you hoped for crumble as you watch Jesus hang like a common criminal on a cross. You wonder: was this man no more than a charismatic personality? Are you to return to business as usual? Imagine visiting the tomb with the women after the Sabbath is over, going there to anoint the body of Jesus—then, finding the tomb empty. Confused and afraid, you wonder, where is he?

"Don't be afraid," an angel tells you. "He is risen from the dead!"

You hurry with the women to tell the other disciples.

If we can imagine the excitement of that first proclamation of the gospel, the Good News, we will have some understanding of how the word of God is to be proclaimed.

Those first disciples knew they were proclaiming Good News. The *Acts of the Apostles* gives us the accounts of their early preaching. Word quickly spread by people telling each other what they had seen and heard. Today, we can read the Good News on printed pages. However, only when that Word takes flesh in us, in our hearts—as it did in the disciples—can we *proclaim* to others that *he is risen, as he said.* The key word here is "proclaim." When we gather to celebrate the word, we are not simply reading what is written; we are proclaiming Christ is present with us here and now, risen as he said.

Our children live in a world that all too often surrounds them with broken promises, empty dreams and false security. Each Sunday Jesus wants them to hear anew that he is with them. He is the one God promised. He is true to his word. How we proclaim this word to children in ritual profoundly influences their sense of God's promise being fulfilled in their lives.

First of all, the children should see that the book of Sunday readings is a special book. It is God's own word. As the symbol of God's presence, it is carried and held with great reverence. The persons who proclaim the word will have reflected beforehand and prayed over the readings so that the word proclaimed is part of their being.

Every proclamation of the word should engage the children. This means that the readers call attention not to themselves but to the text. Is the reading poetry, a story, a dialogue with different characters? While the reading may be adapted in language children understand, the text must also be read with expression and in a manner that draws the children into the life that the word conveys.

We won't want to rush through the readings. We must always remember that these words are God's self-revelation. It is not we who are speaking; rather, God is speaking through us. What God has to say is infinitely more important than what we may say. So take time to read in a manner that engages the children and helps them to understand what God has to say. Let the children see by the way you hold the book and turn its pages that there is more here than eye can see and ear can hear.

Let silence speak of God's presence. It is often appropriate to allow for a little quiet after the first reading. Allow time for the word to touch the children's hearts before inviting them to respond in song or after their song response.

The gospel is pre-eminently the Good News of Jesus Christ. While all of Sacred Scripture has been given for our benefit, the gospel is the Good News of our salvation.

We symbolize—dramatize—our belief in the Risen Lord by standing to hear the proclamation of the gospel. The gospel is joyfully announced with the singing of the "Alleluia." With the same joyful attitude we proclaim—and not just read—the gospel. Imagine how you would proclaim the gospel if you were one of the original disciples, among the first to tell that Good News to others.

The proclamation of the word should have all the drama and excitement that truly conveys God's desire to be part of our lives, to walk and talk and laugh and cry with us. As you proclaim the word, be attentive to the faces of the children. Their expressions will reveal God's word alive in them.

Children are naturally curious about life's mysteries. They wonder about great truths revealed in the scriptures. While we are reading the scriptures, the children are "reading" us—sensing what we feel, absorbing the sense of wonder we convey in our manner.

While we profoundly influence how children receive the word, we need to be aware that each child's life experience also influences how the child hears God's word. When reflecting on the word with children, we show sensitivity to their experience by listening first to what they have heard God say to them. We must resist the temptation to rush in and tell the children what the word is supposed to mean to them. The Word speaks to each of us individually. We must respect the meaning that the Word reveals in each person's life. That meaning is God's own self-revelation.

The key—the absolutely indispensable key—to celebrating the word with children is to avoid getting in the way of God's revelation to them. Children hear the word in an uncomplicated way. The word enters their open hearts without barriers borne of sophistication. They truly believe, as we must believe if we are being true to the Word, that God desires and does speak to them personally.

When celebrating the word with children, our training in pedagogy does not always serve us well. We want to teach rather than letting God speak. We tend to impose upon children what we have heard as adults, ignoring the fact that children have a spiritual life that grows from within as much as from outside influences.

We need, therefore, to know what they have heard. Usually they are eager to tell us. All we need do is ask a simple question: "What did you hear?" Or, "What did you hear God (or Jesus) say?" Most children, in their response, will repeat back a line of the gospel or tell a little of the story. After several children have responded, the gospel has been nearly repeated.

In addition to repeating the gospel, some children will say such things as, "I heard God say . . . ," and then they'll tell you amazing things. Often children will focus on the "message" rather than the story line. We show reverence for those revelations by avoiding the tendency to "correct" or "refine" what children express is the "message" to them. Better to explore with them, to encourage them to reflect further, to see what they come to discover.

Following these reflections on what we have heard God say to us, we reflect upon how the gospel of the day might relate to our daily lives. Children can be particularly perceptive in their application of the gospel to their lives. They are not only articulate; they are ready to act on what they say.

The gospel is a call to conversion for both children and adults. But can children really understand the gospel and experience its call to conversion? One personal experience in celebrating the word with children illustrates how dynamically God can and does work in the hearts of children.

We were reflecting on the gospel for the 3rd Sunday in Ordinary Time (Year C). This is that wonderful account about Jesus returning to Nazareth, reading in the synagogue and proclaiming the text from *Isaiah* to be his own "job description." It says, in part: "The Spirit of God is upon me. God has anointed me and sent me to bring Good News to the poor, to proclaim freedom to those who are oppressed by others, to give sight to the blind, and to announce a special time of blessing from God" (*Luke* 4: 14-21).

After the children echoed back what they had heard, we began to talk about what this gospel might mean in their lives. One child said that being oppressed means "like when someone is down and can't get up alone or like when nobody likes one of the children and the child doesn't have any friends." Another said that we could free the oppressed person by making friends and sitting at the lunch table or playing together. They spoke of "bringing Good News" by letting everyone know we love them. Then something I'll never forget happened.

Manny, a beautiful, dark-haired, dark-eyed little boy said in a somewhat distant voice, "Jesus wants us to love even people who shoot people?"

The question was not addressed as much to me as it was to the gospel itself. I asked, "What do you think, Manny?"

He repeated what he had said with exactly the same quizzical tone of voice. He was looking for an answer that he seemed to know was not an easy one.

I said, "That's hard, isn't it, Manny?"

He didn't answer.

Felton did. He turned to Manny and said, "It's hard. It's really hard, but Jesus said that we have the Spirit of the Lord on us, so we have the power of the Spirit to help us."

What I did not know—though some of the children knew—was that Manny's father had been shot and killed.

What was happening in this celebration?

A seven-year-old child heard the gospel—God's word—and was confronting the struggle we call *conversion*, with the support of a young companion.

Not all children respond immediately to the invitation, "What did you hear?" So we need to allow time for the children to reflect. By our own reflective manner and tone of voice, we can encourage even the more timid children to feel secure in sharing their thoughts. If, after a reverent silence, we sense that the children have not encountered with the word, we respectfully take up the book of readings again and, once more, slowly read the text, remaining attentive to the children as we reflect with them on the word.

This approach to proclaiming and reflecting on the word is one of many. We need to vary from time to time but always in a way that complements the particular text. Whatever our approach, we must always allow the word to resonate in the children themselves. With that principle in mind, here are several examples.

The simplest and most direct method is to ask questions and elicit the children's responses. You might prepare a list of questions beforehand, though you may want to make changes in the course of the reflection. Here are several questions related to the story of Zacchaeus, 31st Sunday of Ordinary Time, Year C. Of course, you need not ask every question.

First, the children listen to the story.

We then help the children examine the story in their terms.

- What did you hear?
- Who will tell me something about this story?
- Where did it all happen? What time of the day did it happen?
- Who were the people there? What were their names?
- What were they doing?
- What did they say?
- Who was the special person in the story?
- Where was he? Why was he there?
- Who was the most important person in the story? What did that person do?
- Something changed between the beginning and the ending of the story; what was it?

The leader guides the children to make the gospel their own, to take God's word to heart.

- What does this story tell us about Jesus?
- How does Jesus treat people?
- What do you think he wants us to know today?
- What can we do?

Some children are quicker than others at answering and contributing their thoughts. Others are more reserved while still others simply enjoy attention. Our

manner will create a sense of respect and mutual support
among the children for each other. Gently calm the
over-eager and keep an eye open for the shy ones who
otherwise never seem to get in a word.

Here is another example, reflecting on the gospel of
the First Sunday of Advent, Year B.

"Jesus said to his disciples,

'Stay awake! Always be ready!
You do not know when your Lord is coming.

'You know that if the owners of a house knew
at what time of night a thief was coming,
they would stay awake
and would not allow the thief to break into their house.

'Well, in the same way, you must always be ready
because you do not know the time
when the Lord is coming.' "

(*Matthew* 24: 42-44)

By questioning the children, guide them in a reflection
about how they get ready for special occasions. A birthday
or Christmas are good examples. We can get ready because
we know the date of Christmas and the date of a birthday.
As the gospel tells us, if we knew when a thief was going to
break into our house, we would be ready.

Now, guide the children's reflections on the great event
for which Jesus wants us to get ready. It is the time when
he will come again. Since we do not know that date, what
must we do? Right: be ready all of the time. Of course,
the children may have a variety of ways of saying this.
Guided by their response, we ask what does it mean to the
children to be ready when Jesus comes? What would you
like to be doing when Jesus comes?

Following this reflection, call the children's attention
to the reading from *Isaiah* for that Sunday:

"The time is coming when everyone will know the house
of God. People of all nations will say,

'Come, let us go to the house of God
so that we may learn to follow God's ways.'

'God will decide what is right for the people.
When that day comes, countries will not fight
against each other anymore. Instead, people
will take their swords and make them into tools
for farming the land. They will take their spears
and make them into tools for pruning trees.
And there will never be war again.

'O people of God, come.
Let us walk in the light of God.' "

(Isaiah 2:1-5)

Isaiah tells us about the special time of the coming.
What will it be like? He says there will be no war, no
fighting, because everyone will be doing things God's way,
which is the way of peace. So we can get ready for Jesus by
making peace, not war. Obviously, children are not
responsible for world conflicts, so we encourage them to
express "making peace, not war" in their own terms, their
own lives. What we do prepares the way for the second
coming of Jesus. We don't know when that will be, but we
can get ready for it by sharing peace and joy at home,
school, with our friends, and especially with those who are
not so friendly.

Here is another example, aimed at helping children get
in touch with the *feelings* of the story. In this case, the
gospel is from the 5th Sunday of Lent, Year C, *John* 8:1-11.
It is about the Pharisees who brought before Jesus the
woman who had been caught committing adultery. You are
familiar with the story.

As you are aware, you will need to explain the meaning
of adultery and the seriousness with which the Jewish
community considered it. That will not be easy, not only
because of the children's varied ages, but also because
today, in some circles, and so evidenced on television and
in films, adultery is often considered the norm. Only in its
proper context can we appreciate the woman's fearful

situation and the gratuitous forgiveness of Jesus.

Involve the children in the mood and feelings of the people in the story. Read the story again slowly to the line, *"They made her stand in front of everyone."*

- Help the children imagine the woman standing in front of an angry crowd eager to stone her.

Then read slowly to the line, *"What should we do with her?"*

- Ask the children how people in the crowd felt.
- How did the woman feel?
- What did she do? Do you think she looked at Jesus? At the crowd?

Read slowly to the line, *"Then Jesus knelt down and wrote on the ground again (the second time)."*

- Now how did the woman feel? Toward the crowd? Toward Jesus?

Read slowly to the line, *"I don't punish you either. Go now and don't sin again."*

- How did the woman feel at this moment?
- How would you feel?
- Do you think her life changed? How? Why?

Although this story seems to be "for adults only," we can use it to reflect with children on the liberating feeling of forgiveness, on being loved by Jesus not just when we do what is right, but even when we do what is wrong.

These are but a few approaches to reflecting on the word with children. You will discover others suited to your particular children. After praying, reflecting privately and with others on the scriptures, letting the Word take flesh in you, then you can trust in the Spirit to help you guide the children by becoming one with them—to whom, Jesus said, the kingdom of heaven belongs.

Discussion Questions

1. How do the various members of the children's liturgy team prepare for the Sunday celebrations? How do

we help one another? How can we nurture the biblical spirituality of our team?

2. How can we improve our proclamations of the word? How well do our styles complement the various literary forms of the readings?

3. What are some of the characteristics of the way we nurture the response of the children to God's word? How do we show our respect for what the children have heard God say to them?

4. What value is there in the quiet moments of our celebrations? Are we comfortable with such silences? Do we proclaim the word and facilitate the children's reflections to accommodate appropriate moments of quiet reflection?

5. How sensitive are we to our inclination to want to make sure the children "learn something," or "get something out of" the celebration?

6. What methods have we found most helpful in nurturing the children's response to God's word?

7. How do we reflect in our celebrations an awareness that children already enjoy a special relationship with God, that they already have a spiritual life?

Chapter 10

BUT WHAT MIGHT
THE CHILDREN HEAR?

As we gather children to hear the scriptures read in language they can understand, we need to ask the question: "What are they hearing?" The question, expressed in one way or another, actually goes back to ancient times and applies to adults as well as to children.

In his foreword to the SUNDAY *Lectionary For Children,* scripture scholar Carroll Stuhlmueller, C.P. writes: "Rabbis and teachers were cautiously but continuously bringing the text of the Bible into communication with the assembly just as the SUNDAY *Lectionary* does for an assembly of children at church today. The Jewish teachers added a long series of changes in the margin of the Bible, indicating what was to be said aloud when this or that word was read silently in the sacred text itself . . . . This practice of adapting the Bible for reading, study and prayer continued in the long tradition of the church."

The *Directory for Masses With Children* is also concerned with what the children might hear: "In the choice of readings the criterion to be followed is the quality rather than the quantity of the texts from the scriptures. In itself a shorter reading is not always more suited to children than a lengthy reading. Everything depends upon the spiritual advantage which the reading can offer to children" (Paragraph 44).

Even when you use a lectionary especially prepared for

children, you will need to reflect upon the way a particular reading might be heard by the particular children with whom you are gathering. Clearly, the experience and the child's *perception* of experience will vary considerably from one familial, cultural or socio-economic setting to the next.

Consider the gospel reading from *Luke* 6:43-45 for the 8th Sunday in Ordinary Time, Year C:

"Jesus said to his disciples,

'Good trees give good fruit
and bad trees give bad fruit.
You don't see figs growing on
bushes with thorns.
No, they grow on fig trees.
And grapes don't grow on
bramble bushes,
but only on grape vines.

'It is the same with human beings.
People who have a good and
kind heart do good things.
But people who have evil
in their hearts do evil things.
People show what is truly
in their hearts
and how they truly are
by what they do.' "

Sounds like a straightforward reading. Nothing particularly obscure or subtle in it. A simple, definitive comparison, based upon experience understandable by both rural as well as urban children whose exposure to fruit trees and grape vines is limited. No problems with this reading, one might think. But what about the experience children are bringing—not of fruit trees, but of significant people in their lives?

Let's say you have 30 children in your gathering for the Liturgy of the Word. Given national averages, a certain percentage—estimates are one in three to five—of those children are likely to have been emotionally and/or

physically abused by their parents or guardians. Listen to
the reading with the ears of these children.

"Good trees give good fruit,
    and bad trees give bad fruit . . . .
    It's the same with human beings . . . ."

What do you think abused children, given their
experience, might be hearing?

Family therapists tell us that children who are
emotionally and/or physically abused believe they have
done something wrong. They think they're bad, otherwise
their parent or guardian would treat them kindly. How do
you imagine the reading from *Luke* might be heard by
innocent children who think they're bad? What is
supposed to be Good News may be received as bad news by
such children. What's a leader to do?

Chances are, we do not know enough about the familial
or personal experiences of the children in our gatherings
to know what variety of interpretations they might be
giving the readings. What's more, God's word says
different things to different people, each of which may be
equally valid—unless you're an absolutist or fundamentalist.
Nevertheless, we can rest assured that Jesus did not
intend to say to abused children that they're bound to do
bad things because they perceive of themselves to be bad.

The example from *Luke* points out the need for leaders
not only to reflect on the meaning of the scriptures so that
our reflections with children are true to the texts; we must
also reflect on the texts from within the experience of the
children. Then we will be better able to help them relate
the story of their lives to the biblical story of God's life
with us. This does not mean that we should tell them
what they are supposed to hear and make the connections
for them.

We want to avoid our adult tendency to make sure the
children get the point—which often is not so much *the*
point as it is *our* point. Our dedication to teach the
children some thing conspires against us—and against
God's own creative word. That Word is creative beyond our

most profound scientific inquiries, our most expansive
artistic expressions, our wildest imaginings, and our
fondest dreams. Our role is to celebrate that
creativity—that Word taken flesh in us— with children.
We have no right to impose our control over God's creative
word by telling children what they're supposed to hear. Of
course, we have every right to share with the children
what we have heard. However, we do that humbly, as
we do not always walk in the light of God's way. We
share with children what we have heard with profound
respect for what they have heard and often lack the skills
to articulate.

But what of the children whose experience of evil in
the world distorts their ability to hear God's liberating
word? We serve them by getting to know them as well as
we try to get to know the scripture texts that we proclaim.

How do you get to know the children, particularly when
the only time you see them is at the Liturgy of the Word?
Here are a few suggestions:

• Have the same leaders meet often enough with the
children so that children and leaders feel at home with
each other. This does not mean that the same few people
should "do all the work." Some parishes go to the other
extreme; in one instance, twelve leaders were taking turns
meeting with a small group of children once every twelve
Sundays. The better arrangement in this case would be for
each volunteer to be the primary leader at least four weeks
in a row and be a participant occasionally at other times.

Related to establishing a feeling of communion among
those gathered, many Catholic communities face the
problem of large numbers. The more we can reduce the
size of our groups of children (and adults), the better.
However, as we have mentioned elsewhere, breaking large
groups of children into grade levels is not appropriate for
liturgical gatherings which should be intergenerational. In
order to form groups of varying ages, you might divide the
children alphabetically by family name. This method also
keeps children of the same family together.

• While you read the scriptures to the children, read also the children's faces. Both are primary sources of revelation—the word proclaimed and the Word already taken flesh in their lives. Is there sadness there? Joy? Peace? Puzzlement? Turmoil? Tranquility?

• After the word has been proclaimed, first ask the children, "What did you hear?" As this becomes part of your style, children come to share their responses more readily and naturally. Resist the urge to fill with your words the silence that may follow. If no one has anything to say, you may take the book again, handling it with reverence, and slowly read the text again, pausing to allow time for the children to reflect and perhaps respond during this second reading. As the *Directory* points out, "children are genuinely capable of reflection." Therefore, silent reflection is quite appropriate and "should be observed at the proper time as a part of the celebration" (Paragraph 37).

• Consider reflecting first with the children on their lives *before* proclaiming the word. You need not do this every time, but when you think the scripture text placed in the context of the children's experience might be problematic for the children. The reading from *Luke* comparing good and bad fruit trees to good and bad people may be more appropriately presented in this way.

Explore first how the children "read" their lives for you. Set the stage for the coming scripture reading by introducing some related experiences—without invading anyone's privacy—in order to help children broaden the perspective with which they may be interpreting their personal experiences. Such reflecting can cultivate, without prejudicing, the children's perceptions of experience; then the word they hear proclaimed can better nourish their sense of God's presence in their lives.

The *Directory* makes the point: "All elements which will help to understand the readings should be given great consideration so that the children may make the biblical readings their own and may come more and more to appreciate the value of God's word.

"Among these elements are the introductory comments which may precede the readings and help the children to listen better and more fruitfully, either by explaining the context or by introducing the text itself" (Paragraph 47). However, the *Directory* warns, such introductory comments and explanations "should not be merely didactic" (Paragraph 23). In everything we do—including setting the context for hearing God's word—we need to keep in mind that we are celebrating with children not schooling them.

• When you prepare for the coming Sunday, reflect on the readings several days in advance, not just the day or evening before. Let the word "work on you"—take flesh in you—through the week. When you feel at home with the reading, stretch yourself: Imagine what a child might think about the reading. Reflect on the reading from different children's points of view—the child age five, ten, or twelve.

Beyond age, what circumstances surround the child? What's going on in the lives of the children? Imagine yourself seeing with the eyes of children you know, hearing with their ears, feeling what they feel. How might those children already be experiencing God's presence—or feeling God's absence at home, in their neighborhood, or in school?

• Remember that the purpose we serve is to proclaim and celebrate God's word—not ours—both in the readings *and in the lives of the children.* We do this so as to inspire the children to follow their celebration of the word with a wholehearted and heartfilled celebration of the eucharist.

So do we pray: Lord, plant your word in our hearts. Let it bear fruit in us.

Discussion Questions

1. Select a reading and reflect on it from the point of view of what the children might hear. How might a child with a particular handicap understand the reading? A child whose parents are divorced? An abused child?

2. How well do we know the children who attend our celebrations? How can we get to know them better? How important is it that we get to know them?

3. How does the number of different leaders in our parish affect the quality and character of the children's experience of celebrating the word? What is the children's sense of continuity from one celebration to the next?

4. What level of security do the children in our gatherings enjoy? How can we provide the kind of group security needed to free the children to respond? Are they comfortable in speaking from the heart, in contrast to saying things that they think the group will find acceptable?

Chapter 11

CELEBRATING THE WORD WITH MUSIC

Music and singing sometimes frighten away people who might otherwise be natural leaders of children's celebration of the word. We hope our emphasis on music does not suggest to you that without music you cannot celebrate God's presence in the word. Rather, we want to encourage you to incorporate music and singing. It need not complicate your celebration. Children love to sing and, with appropriate music and very little help, they can pick up tunes without rehearsing. Although some of the ideas here may seem beyond you, the secret is: sing God a simple song.

Music is a priority in celebrations of the word with children, and a variety of ways exist to incorporate music simply and effectively. Ideally, the leader has some instrumental training. That's not absolutely necessary. Anyone who can sing reasonably well, with expression, can lead children in song.

Leaders who are not musicians can learn children's music from available recordings. These recordings, however, are not recommended for use during the celebration, even though the intent may be to have the children sing along. Nor do we recommend that you use these recordings during the celebration to practice with the children before they sing the songs on their own. That's not necessary. Preferably, the leader learns the

music beforehand, then leads the children without
depending on a recording. By so doing, the children are
better able to make the ritual their own original expression
of praise.

Also, while live music is always preferred—especially if
performed by the children—recorded instrumental music
can serve to create prayerful, reflective moods. The object,
however, is not to entertain, nor to have children who are
musically inclined perform for the sake of entertaining
others. Rather, the purpose is to enhance the entire
community's own creative expression of praise.

Why is music so important?

Can you imagine a parade without a band? A birthday
party without singing "Happy Birthday"? Christmas
without carols? It is hard to conceive of a celebration or
season without music.

Music is the medium of the spirit. Music puts us in
touch with what lies hidden in human experience. Through
music we can not only recall but *relive* past experiences.

When people make music together, they convey to one
another—and thereby experience in each other—a harmony
of spirit that includes even those who cannot sing on key.
Music unites people. Through music people not only
express their identity but also celebrate the way of life they
share. Polish polkas, Negro spirituals, German "um-pah"
bands . . . each conveys a different attitude toward life.

Little wonder, then, that music plays a vital part in
ritual- making and our liturgical rites. In liturgy, we
convey a unique attitude toward life. In liturgy, we not
only recall, we *relive* the paschal mystery. In liturgy, we
not only express our identity as Christians, we celebrate
the life of Christ we share through the power of the Holy
Spirit. Without music we really cannot do very well what
we claim to do in liturgy.

Therefore, when we celebrate the word with children
we use music. We sing. We make sounds of joy and praise.
We move to the rhythm of the spirit. In these ways we not
only recall the words of God revealed throughout human

history, we *relive* God's own presence—God's own Word made flesh—in human experience. Of course, children do not rationalize or analyze their liturgical experiences in this way. Nonetheless, they can and do experience the presence of God that music awakens and celebrates.

Drawing from the "General Instruction of the Roman Missal," the *Directory* observes, "Singing is of great importance in all celebrations, but it is to be especially encouraged in every way for Masses celebrated with children, in view of their special affinity for music. The culture of various groups and the capabilities of the children present should be taken into account . . . .

"The use of 'musical instruments may be of great help' in Masses with children, especially if they are played by the children themselves. The playing of instruments will help to support the singing or to encourage the reflection of the children; sometimes by themselves instruments express festive joy and the praise of God" (Paragraphs 30 & 32).

Everything we've said so far has aimed to answer the question, "Why is music so important?" Another question often asked is: "What kind of music should we use?"

The obvious answer, of course, is music that children can sing. However, this is not as simple as it sounds. Not only does the melody need to be simple and singable, it also needs to communicate the spirit of the text. Moreover, the text needs to be uncluttered and biblically sound—in other words, of lasting value.

Music has a powerful effect on children long after childhood. Children learn more quickly and retain for much longer ideas put to music rather than those expressed in words memorized by rote. Who will ever forget the ABC song? Those of us, moreover, who cut our vocal chords on Gregorian Chant long remember Latin lyrics we didn't understand for many years. With music, children carry their response to God's word in their hearts for a lifetime.

Music appropriate for children's Liturgy of the Word needs to be brief and flexible in its design. Lengthy hymns, for example, tend to slow celebrations down. With brief responses and acclamations, children can sing not only between readings but also within the proclamation of the reading itself. This may seem too advanced for you to try when you're still beginning to celebrate the word with children. If so, keep it in mind as something to work toward. Also, this is something you would do only if the reading lends itself to such a proclamation. Consider, for example, celebrating the proclamation of the gospel for the 9th Sunday in Ordinary Time (Year A) by interspersing the acclamation, with music by Christopher Walker, like this:

Leader: This is a reading from the Gospel of Matthew.

Children: (*Singing first line of acclamation.*)
          Listen to Jesus. Alleluia.
          Listen and do what he says.

Leader: Jesus said to his disciples,
          "It isn't enough just to call me the Lord
          without doing what God says.
          The people who will enter heaven are the
          ones who do what God wants them to do."

Children: (*Singing second line of acclamation
          with slight musical variation from first line.*)
          Listen to Jesus. Alleluia.
          Listen and do what he says.

Leader: Then Jesus gave them this example:
"Anyone who hears my words and does
what I say is like a wise person
who builds a house on solid ground.
When it rains and the wind blows very hard,
or when a flood comes, the house will not
fall down because it is built on rock.

Children: *(Singing first line, again, of acclamation.)*
Listen to Jesus. Alleluia.
Listen and do what he says.

Leader: "But anyone who hears my words
but doesn't do what I say is like
a foolish person who builds a house on sand.
When it rains hard or there is a flood
or the wind is too strong,
the house will fall down
because it was only built on sand."

Children: *(Singing second line, again, of acclamation.)*
Listen to Jesus. Alleluia.
Listen and do what he says.

By integrating the music with the proclamation, the children themselves actively share in proclaiming the word. They are celebrating the word and responding as they hear it.

With music that is brief, children pick up the melody quickly and enjoy the repetition. What's more, children don't have to rehearse. More is lost than gained when we practice music during celebration time. We lose the movement and mood of the celebration when, following our procession to hear the word proclaimed, we stop for singing practice. Also, we really don't remember what little we may have learned from practice, surely not enough to make any real difference in our participation, nor enough to pay the price of breaking the mood and movement of the celebration.

While children are quick to learn music, they also enjoy singing familiar melodies. For example, the music

Christopher Walker wrote for use during Advent in the
SUNDAY Liturgy of the Word series repeats the same
melody from one Sunday to the next. However, the words
change to complement the content of each Sunday's
readings. Such music, while familiar to the children from
Sunday to Sunday, helps sustain a mood for an entire
liturgical season.

Still another question: "When are the appropriate
times to use music?"

As with parades, the children's procession from the
main assembly calls for music. In some parishes, the
entire assembly stands to sing the processional song with
the children as they leave for their celebration of the word.
The assembly's participation gives recognition to the
celebration of the word with children as an integral part of
the main assembly's celebration.

As the children's procession leaves the assembly, the
song leader walks at the beginning rather than at the end
of the procession. Then, as the children enter their place
of celebration, the sound of music is filling the room. If
the song leader walks at the end of the procession,
children who are first to enter the separate celebration
space may not be able to sustain the song. Ideally, several
adults or "shepherds" know the music and position
themselves throughout the procession.

If the children are not singing while in procession,
instrumental music may be used to create a mood of
reverence in the separate celebration space. The melody
of this music might be taken from the response and/or the
gospel acclamation for that Sunday. Playing these melodies
then both sets the mood and indirectly introduces the
children to the music they will later be singing.

Whenever possible, the children themselves should be
encouraged to play musical instruments, either as part of
the processional or to enhance the celebration itself.
Flutes, bells or chimes, recorders, ocarinas, bongo drums,
tambourines, and other rhythm instruments provide a
variety of sounds to express a range of moods that

complement the various feasts and liturgical seasons.

Musical instruments can "set the stage" for a reading, serving to focus the children's attention or build anticipation for what is to happen next. Similarly, instrumental music can support periods of meditation, or guide the group into and out of moments of silence.

Furthermore, instrumental sounds can heighten the dramatic effect of certain readings. An obvious example is during the reading of the gospel on Passion Sunday, or a dramatic reading of the Passion as provided in the *SUNDAY Lectionary for Children*. A slow, elongated, rhythmic striking of a bongo drum would reinforce the dramatic impact of Jesus' passion and death.

It is particularly important to use music with the response and gospel acclamation. This is not to say the song leader or a song group sings these while the children listen. The children sing these and, as we mentioned earlier, the children need not practice them. The composition of the response, for example, usually includes a refrain and several verses. The leader simply starts by singing the refrain, which the children repeat. Then the leader sings the verses, to which the children respond by singing the refrain again after each verse. By the second verse the children will not only know the music, they will remember it well enough to sing it on the way home.

A note might be worth adding here about how the response might be more properly understood. "Response" is often taken to mean the psalm or song we sing in response to the reading. While it can be taken to mean that, "response" is more properly descriptive of the way in which the psalm or song is to be performed—that is, with a leader or a group of children singing the verses, to which the rest of the children sing in response. Or, you may have different groups of children sing different verses, to which the entire group joins in with the refrain. You might imagine it as a kind of musical juggling act, in which first one group catches the music, then tosses it to another, then perhaps to a third, then back again.

When understood in this way, the response serves not only as a song to sing after the first reading, but as a musical celebration that completely *surrounds* the reading. In some cases, you may even want to repeat the response at appropriate points during the proclamation of the first reading, similar to the example we gave above for the proclamation of the gospel for the 9th Sunday in Ordinary Time (Year A).

Similarly, the gospel acclamation is easy to sing without practice. The leader first sings it alone, then the children repeat it, again and again, not just to make sure everyone is singing, but to build the group's enthusiasm for the Good News to be proclaimed!

Consider, for example, the 19th Sunday in Ordinary Time (Year A). The gospel is about Jesus inviting Peter to walk on water—in a storm, no less! The gospel acclamation reads: "Jesus said: 'Don't be afraid! Come to me.' Alleluia!"

Je-sus said: "Don't be a-fraid! Come to me." Al-le-lu - ia!   lu - ia!

Imagine starting the singing of the gospel acclamation slowly at first, quietly. Then as you repeat it—and more children catch on—the voices grow stronger, more strident and confident.

You can see, given these examples of the way to integrate music and proclamation, that the texture of the Liturgy of the Word with children is one of *celebration*. With music, the entire celebration of the word becomes a ritual drama that, while under the direction of adults, is *performed by the children and adults*.

We need not feel restricted by the prescribed ritual form. Rather, we use the ritual form as a framework within which to encourage the children to flourish in their expressions of praise. We cannot say it often enough to ourselves as we plan and evaluate our celebrations: let the children lead us.

Discussion Questions

1. How do we incorporate music in our celebrations? In the procession? To establish a mood in the worship space? To enhance the children's response?

2. What does music contribute? How can we improve our use of music?

3. Are we making the best use of the musical talent in the parish? Of the children's talents?

4. Have we learned to style our use of music so that we don't feel the need to practice songs with the children before we sing them in the celebration?

5. How well does our selection of music complement the Sunday readings and liturgical seasons? Does our music help the children carry God's word with them in their hearts?

Chapter 12

THE CHILDREN'S PROFESSION OF FAITH AND PRAYER OF THE FAITHFUL

Have you ever watched the eyes of a child at a magic show? Or sat with children as they listen to a story being told? Part of the joy of Christmas is seeing little children in hiding, hoping to catch a glimpse of Santa Claus. Children spontaneously and trustingly believe in a world beyond their understanding and experience.

But what do children believe about God? How do children relate to the deity? Those who have done research in the spirituality of children, particularly Robert Coles, the psychiatrist from Harvard University, tell us that children, regardless of religion or particular training, have a natural belief in Someone beyond themselves. His entire book, *The Spiritual Life of Children* (Houghton Mifflin Company, Boston, 1990), is evidence of children's rich awareness of God's presence in their lives.

Religion and training put that belief in a particular language. In the Roman Catholic tradition, the belief has been summarized in a variety of forms. We are most familiar with the Nicene Creed and the Apostles' Creed, two statements of what the church has come to hold as a summary of faith. On Sundays and solemnities we recite one or the other of these creeds as our Profession of Faith. At the Easter Vigil, we profess our faith in still another form as we renew our baptismal promises. This is the creedal form that we suggest you use with children.

At the Easter Vigil, we are asked a series of questions and invited to respond with "I do."

"Do you believe in God, the Father Almighty, creator of heaven and earth?"

"Do you believe in Jesus Christ, his only Son, our Lord, who was born of the Virgin Mary, was crucified, died and was buried, rose from the dead and is now seated at the right hand of the Father?"

"Do you believe in the Holy Spirit, the holy catholic church, the communion of saints, the forgiveness of sins, the resurrection of the body and life everlasting?"

Notice three points about this form of our Profession of Faith. First, it is set in question and answer form. We listen to the question, then verbalize our response. Second, the form has three parts, each beginning with a different Person of the Trinity: Do you believe in God? Do you believe in Jesus Christ? Do you believe in the Holy Spirit? Third, we add to each of these three Persons other attributions for our affirmative response.

This form, questions and response about the Trinity and the life of the Trinity in our lives seems quite suitable for children. Moreover, it embraces the foundational truths of our faith. But the detailed baptismal creed, as written for adults, is beyond the comprehension of children. How might we adapt it so that children ages 5 to 12 can find meaning there?

Those who have made it a practice to ask children these same questions in language children can understand have found that children quickly—enthusiastically— respond with an unqualified "Yes!" Also, by focusing on the core content of the creed, you can incorporate details that reflect the liturgical season and, when possible, the content of the readings the children just heard. Here is an example of a creed for children during the season of Advent and Christmas:

> *Do you believe that God made you, loves you, and calls you by name?*
> *Do you believe that Jesus was born of the Virgin Mary*

by the power of the Holy Spirit?
Do you believe that Jesus is the Son of God?
Do you believe that Jesus came to earth to teach us how to live and how to love?
Do you believe that the Holy Spirit lives in our hearts and helps us to live the way Jesus wants us to live?

You will notice that this variation emphasizes the birth of Jesus. Obviously, more can be said and should be said about God as Creator and about the death and resurrection of Jesus, and about the Holy Spirit. With children, it is not necessary to say everything, every time we profess our faith. However, throughout the liturgical year, other variations will emphasize the entire content of the creed. Here is an example of a children's creed for the Lenten/Easter Seasons:

Do you believe that God made you, loves you, and calls you by name?
Do you believe that Jesus was born of the Virgin Mary and came to teach us how to live and how to love?
Do you believe that Jesus suffered and died on a cross because he loves us?
Do you believe that Jesus rose from the dead and is living with us?
Do you believe that Jesus will come some day to take us to heaven and that we will live with him forever?
Do you believe that the Holy Spirit lives in our hearts and helps us to live the way Jesus wants us to live?

During the season of Ordinary Time, we celebrate the life and ministry of Jesus on earth. During this season, we hear our call to become disciples and to follow Jesus. The scriptures describe the ministry of Jesus in miracle stories, parables, personal relationships. In each of these, God invites us to respond. Here is an example of a children's creed for use during Ordinary Time:

Do you believe that God made you, loves you, and calls you by name?

Do you believe that Jesus was born of the Virgin Mary and came to teach us to live and how to love?
Do you believe that Jesus can do all things and wants to heal and teach all people? (This line can take its content from the gospel of the day. On the Fifth Sunday (Year A), for instance, you might say, *"Do you believe that you are the light of the world and the salt of the earth?"* Or, for the 17th Sunday (Year A), *"Do you believe that Jesus wants us to love people who are not kind to us?"*)
Do you believe that Jesus wants us to be his disciples and to follow him? (If disciples or others are named in the readings, you might add their names or anyone whom the gospel might mention. For example, *"Do you believe that Jesus wants us to be his disciples and to follow Jesus like the man Jesus cured of blindness?"* Or, *"like Peter and Andrew?"* Or, *"like James and John?"*)
Do you believe that the Holy Spirit lives in our hearts and helps us to live the way Jesus wants us to live?

Of course, during the time of Pentecost as well as on Sundays that speak particularly about the Spirit—the Twelfth or Twenty-third Sundays of Ordinary Time, Year C— you might lengthen the section on the Holy Spirit. On the other hand, you can emphasize the First Person of the Trinity on such Sundays as the Twelfth Sunday of Ordinary Time in Year B, the Second Sunday in Ordinary Time Year A, and the Fourth Sunday of Ordinary Time in Year C. Each of these emphasizes God as creator of an individual or of nature. In this case, you might ask:

Do you believe that God made you, loves you and calls you by name?
Do you believe that you are special to God and that God always takes care of you?
Do you believe that God made all people and loves each one very much?
Do you believe that God made everything—the

animals, the trees, the mountains and oceans?
Do you believe that Jesus was born of the Virgin Mary
and came to teach us about God and to show us who
God is?
Do you believe the Holy Spirit lives in our hearts and
helps us to live the way Jesus wants us to live?

Each of the creeds might end with such words as:

This is what our church teaches and what we believe,
so we all say, "Amen!"
"Amen!"

As you prepare for each Sunday's readings, you will
know what to emphasize in the creed. One guideline: keep
the statements short so that the children can easily grasp
and respond to them. Also, limit the number of questions
to fewer than six. You will notice that in each of the
adapted creeds, three questions remain the same so that
the children always profess their faith in God as Creator,
Son and Holy Spirit. The point is: the creed should always
be Trinitarian and should invite the children to express
their belief in the word of God they've just heard.

The Prayer of the Faithful

Having professed our faith in creedal form, we now
express our faith through our concern for others. The
Prayer of the Faithful, like the creed, should take its cue
from the readings of the day. For example, when we read
about Jesus healing the sick, we will want to invite the
children to pray especially for those who are sick. When
we hear of Jesus' concern for the poor, the hungry, the
marginal members of society, we will want to invite the
children to pray for those in need.

We need to keep in mind that the leader's role is to
guide *the children to pray in their own words* rather than
mention a list of items to which the children give their
assent. The children themselves are given an opportunity
to pray for people they know personally, situations that
concern their families, their friends, their parish and

neighborhood. At the same time, we want to raise the consciousness of children to the human condition of the larger community. Especially will older children be aware of problems beyond their local community and in the world at large. In either case, we need to encourage the children by our example to be concrete—as young children will be naturally—and focused so that the prayer is truly *their prayer.*

Moreover, it should be noted that the Prayer of the Faithful is a single prayer with several intentions and is not a series of separate prayers.

It begins with an invitation to pray, addressed by the leader to the children. The leader can do this quite simply by making use of a key phrase from the gospel of the day. For example, the First Sunday of Advent, Year C:

> *Jesus said, "Always be ready! Stay awake!" Let us pray that we will always be ready to hear God's voice and never get tired of doing what God asks.*

The intentions that follow are calls to the children to pray privately for particular needs, people, situations and so forth. Again, they are addressed to the children, not to God. For example:

> *Let us pray for people who are sick, especially for Jane's daddy.*

The intentions will naturally reflect the children's own needs and interests. To broaden their horizons, the leader may need to add one or two universal intentions. As mentioned earlier, this should be the prayer of the children. They should be encouraged to formulate and express their intentions, either by writing them down, or by speaking spontaneously. A phrase is all that the leader needs to encourage children:

> *Is there anyone else we want to pray for? What about the people we saw on TV whose houses were destroyed by the tornado?*

A short silence follows each intention so that the

children can reflect on their personal prayer. This is most important because silence allows the children to pray in their own ways. Moreover, silence helps communicate the presence of God with us.

A response concludes each moment of personal prayer, such as, "Lord, hear our prayer." In this way, the diverse prayers of many individuals are gathered and become the prayer of the community.

A sung response to the Prayer of the Faithful can unify the prayer intentions of the children. After the intention has been said, there should be a moment of silence for private prayers; then the leader sings and the children respond.

The leader concludes the entire prayer with a collect, addressed to God on behalf of the children. The leader may also use the Prayer of the Day, presented each week in the SUNDAY Celebration of the Word materials. Some leaders may prefer a simpler, closing formula, such as: *We make this and all our prayers through Christ our Lord.*

If time is limited, the leader should conclude with at least a brief prayer. The following example is broadly adapted from the Opening Prayer:

Leader:
Let us pray that we will get ready for the coming of Jesus. (Pause for silent prayer.)

Response (expressed by leader):
God who made us,
you are full of kindness and peace.
Help us always to be ready for Jesus
when he comes, and make us brave
to do what is right and peaceful.
We ask you this through Jesus, your Son,
who lives and reigns forever and ever.

All: *Amen.*

One final thought: an unvaried children's celebration of the word that uses only simplified readings and prayer texts may be little more than an adult celebration in modified language. Children need more than verbal involvement. They need also to express themselves in the language of gesture and movement.

Gestures to accompany a prayer embody the words of that prayer. The basic raising of open, outstretched hands by all the children is a most effective gesture. Standing, sitting, kneeling, closing eyes, and clasping hands are a few among many possibilities. Adults who participate in the children's celebration and other older children should be aware that they serve—through their prayerful attitude and bodily expressions—as models for the younger children. In other words, the best way to teach children to pray is not so much through instruction but through the way we pray with them.

Discussion Questions

1. Describe the basic characteristics and content of a creed for children.

2. Are we familiar with the creedal statements that are suitable for use with the children? If not, how can we develop such familiarity?

3. Prepare several creeds for use with children by following the guidelines outlined in this chapter. Practice them with each other.

4. How does what we proclaim in the creed affect the children, keeping in mind the various experiences of the children?

5. Describe the basic characteristics of the Prayer of the Faithful for children.

6. How do we draw our Prayers of the Faithful from the children?

7. Design some Prayers of the Faithful that are based upon different Sunday readings but that also solicit reflections from the children.

Chapter 13

CELEBRATING GOD'S WORD IN THE HOME

Often we hear the home described as "the little church." The expression attempts to place a symbolic value on families that we might not otherwise recognize. Presumably, then, "the *big* church" is the parish. Does that make one more important than the other?

Such measurements of apparent importance based upon size reminds me of a reflection the late poet and columnist John Ciardi entertained while driving down a Michigan highway where he came upon a sign pointing to a side road:

"THIS WAY TO THE WORLD'S LARGEST CRUCIFIX."

Such a grand claim caused Ciardi to wonder: In what sense can the world's largest crucifix be any larger than the world's smallest crucifix? In what sense is the world's largest act of love any larger than the world's smallest? The largest act of kindness any larger than the smallest?

Size cannot measure such matters, Ciardi concluded. He did not turn down the side road.

We need to avoid turning down the side road to "the world's largest church." "The little church" is no smaller than the world's "largest church." Nor was the two disciples' supper at the family-operated Emmaus Inn any smaller than the feast of five thousand on the hillsides of the Sea of Galilee.

When we nurture the home church, we nurture the universal church.

But what's happening in homes today?

Item: Myriam Miedzian reports in her book *Boys Will Be Boys* (Doubleday 1991) that American children view TV approximately 24 hours per week. By the time they're 18, children have viewed 26,000 murders on the screen.

Item: According to the US Census Bureau (*US News & World Report*, December 16, 1991), 3.2-million children live with their grandparents—an increase of almost 40% in the past decade.

Item: The *Child Welfare Journal* (Jan.-Feb. issue, 1992) reports that 3,000 children's lives are disrupted by a divorce *on an average day* in the United States.

Item: The "Hearing Before the Subcommittee on Children" (Government Document No. Y 4.L11/4.102-43, page 6) reveals that *in one day in the lives of American children*:

- 1,849 children are abused;
- 16 commit suicide;
- 3,288 run away from home;
- 1,500 teens drop out of school;
- 135,000 children bring a gun to school;
- 7,742 teens become sexually active;
- 2,795 teens get pregnant;
- 1,295 teens give birth.

Item: The 4th Edition of "Child Welfare: Policies & Practices" (Costin, Bell, Downs, 1991) reports:

- Ten million latch-key children in the United States.
- 96% of 13-year-olds go home to an empty house.
- 76% of 12-year-olds go home to an empty house.
- 82% of 11-year-olds go home to an empty house.

Families in our society are under unprecedented stress. How well do our parish religious education programs and Christian initiation efforts reflect the reality of family life today? Whose needs are our programs really serving? Do our parish programs operate with an awareness of what's happening in the lives of children today or within the context of some other "reality"?

What influence do your parish liturgical celebrations have on the lives of your parish's families today? What significance can church-related rituals have in family-life today?

The influence of church-related rituals on children—and adults—today can be measured by the extent to which parents and children take ownership of the rites. That is one of the profound—albeit long-ranged—potential impacts that the children's Liturgy of the Word promises. When children see their mothers and fathers and other adults serve in a role traditionally reserved for the ordained clergy, the children's image of the church changes. What's more, both children and parents have an opportunity to experience a sense of ownership of the rituals that has not been available to them in the same way before.

Such ownership of—and responsibility for—rituals is fundamental to communicating a Christian identity from one generation to the next. That is what ritual does. Each family—whether it be single-parented or working-parented or grand-parented—will have its own rituals that provide the family its identity. The way we celebrate holidays, anniversaries or birthdays—the special family recipes that we fix and pass on from one generation to the next—give our family its identity. It gives the children a way of saying who they are. Little everyday rituals—the way our family members begin and end each day together and in their smaller gestures of "good-morning" and "good-night," "hello" and "goodbye"—often serve as signs of continuity or conflict in the flow of our lives together.

Church-related rituals have the same potential to give children and adults who take ownership of them a sense of Christian identity, of belonging to God's own family. That is a critical need of children and adults: to know that they belong, that someone cares what happens to them, that they are not just anybody but *somebody*.

That is the "bottom line" in God's family "economy of salvation": each of us counts. God calls each person by

name. That's Good News to fragile families afloat in a
technological, profit-centered—rather than people-
centered—"economy of secularization." All of us—adults
and children—need to be reassured over and over again of
God's care for us. We do that through ritual-making,
through celebrating God's Good News over and over again;
similarly, parents and children need to tell each other over
and over again that they care for each other and to
celebrate that care through ritual recognition of
significant events—happy and sad—and in the mini-rites
we follow to mark the beginning and ending of each day.

There is a growing awareness, not only in the church
but also in society, of the significance of ritual-making in
our lives today. The suggestions that follow for nurturing
the celebration of God's word in the home reflect the need
for ritual-making to be every parish's priority. The point
here is not to argue the relative merits of traditional
classroom teaching and the formative impact of initiation
rituals. We can nurture family life with God's word
through our schools and religious education programs as
well as through liturgies of the word with children when
the parish gathers on weekends.

We just need to re-examine our present practices.

Parents Are Models

Parents—or the child's significant adults—are the most
powerful symbols to children. What we stand for in the
eyes of our children profoundly influences our children's
attitudes toward life.

Faith is an attitude. It is our inner disposition with
which we relate to others, find meaning in life, and give
meaning to our experience.

Adults soon discover that when they have children
their attitude toward life changes. The experience can so
threaten some adults that they struggle against the
change. On the other hand, for those willing to take
advantage of it, the experience offers adults an
opportunity to explore and learn more about life *through*
their children, that is, to grow with them by looking at life

through their eyes. The children of such parents thereby discover within themselves a spirituality—born of their parents' looking at life through the children's eyes—that is curious and respectful of what lies hidden not only in life outside but also in the life within themselves. This is the door to wonder and awe. The benefits to such children are reciprocal for their parents—and for the entire adult community. This is organic to the process of initiating children into the Christian community.

In other words, the quality of the children's experience of Christian initiation can be measured by the extent to which the process nurtures the entire community's spiritual life. This is the kind of reciprocal modeling that parents (adults) and children provide each other when they pray together and celebrate the presence of God's word proclaimed and the Word made flesh in them.

Through the celebration of the word we look at life with the attitude of Jesus. We do this over and over again because we are constantly changing and the world is constantly changing around us. The ritual process is one in which we are all, every day, being initiated into the life and work of Jesus.

The *Directory* makes this point about parents: "By reason of the responsibility freely accepted at the baptism of their children, parents are bound in conscience to teach them gradually to pray. This they do by praying with them each day and by introducing them to prayers said privately. If children are prepared in this way, even from their early years, and do take part in the Mass with their family when they wish, they will easily begin to sing and to pray in the liturgical community; indeed, they will have some kind of foretaste of the eucharistic mystery" (Paragraph 10).

The task of parish leaders is to help parents enter into this process and provide them with the tools they need to do so.

Serving Parents & Families

There are a variety of ways we can nurture the liturgical spirituality of families.

• The Sunday readings provide a natural focal point for involving busy parents—often employed outside the home—in the religious education of their children. By focusing on the Sunday scriptures, parents are simply encouraged to do what they should be doing anyway as participants in the Sunday liturgy: celebrate God's word, then reflect and respond to it through the week.

To support this involvement, a growing number of parishes are giving families weekly leaflets that contain the Sunday readings adapted for children and carefully illustrated to convey the message of the texts to smaller children who are still learning to read. These leaflets are not to be confused with those that tell you someone else's thoughts *about* the Sunday readings. Such leaflets often get in the way of God's word. What's more, the effort made to apply the scriptures to life are often fabrications that upon thoughtful examination have little to do with the content of God's word and even less to do with the reality of various families' lives.

If we believe God's word is creative—that when God speaks, God creates—then let us proclaim God's word in language children and parents can understand, and get out of the way. This is one of the principles that the SUNDAY family leaflets, for example, apply in their weekly presentation of God's word. The focus is always to nurture the family's own reflections and responses to what they hear God is saying to them. The supporting illustrations are sensitive to the message of the texts, the prayers complement the readings, and the simple reflective activities focus on God's word, not on someone else's reflections on the word nor on some distracting puzzle or word game.

• Some parishes have organized family-centered religious education programs for children under 12 years old. Entire families meet periodically to assume responsibility for preparing their own children for the sacraments. These gatherings are an extension of the weekend celebrations of the word with children.

● Other parishes are supporting the liturgical spirituality of families by sending home with parents ideas on how to celebrate the various feasts and seasons of the church year. Also, parents gather periodically after the Sunday celebrations to exchange ideas with each other not just about extending church-related rituals into their homes, but also about other parenting questions and problems. Simple hospitality serves as the basis for such gatherings and exchanges.

● In some parishes the celebration of the word with children is not possible on weekends. In such cases, parishes with schools are beginning the week with classroom celebrations of the word using the readings of the *previous* Sunday and give the children family scripture leaflets to use at home with their parents.

Some schools prefer to celebrate the Liturgy of the Word on Friday. It makes little difference whether the celebration takes place on Friday or Monday so long as it is a *celebration* and not instruction. The Liturgy of the Word on Monday is not a review to make sure the children understood the readings the day before; and the Liturgy of the Word on Friday is not a preparation to make sure they will understand the word on Sunday. The principles discussed in chapter nine apply wherever and whenever we celebrate the word.

When the Liturgy of the Word is celebrated in a Catholic school classroom or as part of a catechetical program, it should take no more time than the celebration of the word would on a Sunday. More importantly, it should not be confused with a religion lesson. Experience has shown that children, even in a class setting, enjoy celebrating the word when a mood has been created which is different from a regular class atmosphere. The place, the time, the setting are not nearly so important as the children's understanding that we are celebrating the word, not teaching it. The example given in chapter nine of Manny and Felton took place in a second grade classroom in a Catholic school. Our celebration began with a centering song and ended with a baptismal creed exactly as we celebrate on Sunday. The *Directory* encourages frequent celebrations of the word. While celebrating in school and religious education settings do not replace the Sunday celebration, we need not restrict our celebrations of the word with children only to Sunday gatherings.

When the celebration of the word takes place in a school setting on a Friday, the following week might include some liturgical catechesis. This should be distinct from the celebration in which we listen to what the children heard God say to them. Liturgical catechesis is a follow-up to the liturgy itself and should be separated in time so that it does not interfere with God's immediate revelation to the children. Liturgical catechesis follows upon and is based upon the ritual experience and on the readings from the lectionary proclaimed previously in the celebration of the word.

Lectionary-based catechesis is an extension of celebrating the word with children (or young people) and has only recently come into serious discussion among liturgists and catechists. In the meantime, we need to exercise caution so that we do not use liturgy as an instructional method. Materials have yet to be produced that reflect sensitivity to the formative influence of celebrating the word in relation to the catechetical process.

Pulpit Power

Parish priests exert a significant influence on the attitudes of parents toward their family responsibilities. Parents, above all, need encouragement and support.

Parish leaders often wonder if parents really use the material given to them or their children. We worry about having a parish bulletin or a Sunday family scripture leaflet, for example, turn up after mass as litter in the parish parking lot.

Pastors often recommend to parishioners that they read the parish bulletin. Similarly, a brief comment from the pulpit about how families can use family-centered liturgical materials and extend the celebration of the word into the home underscores the value parish leaders place on nurturing a liturgical spirituality in the community.

The problem, again, has to do with encouraging parishioners to take ownership of church-related rites. Many church-goers still believe that, while every effort is made to involve the entire community, the liturgy really belongs to those who are ordained to preside at such functions. They see themselves as participants not performers. Extending the Liturgy of the Word into the home—if done thoughtfully and carefully—can help families discover the riches of the church's liturgical tradition and the power of God's presence in the word to make all things new again.

Discussion Questions

1. How well are we in touch with the families of the children who gather to celebrate the word? What are our opportunities for contact?

2. How are we, as a parish, nurturing the spiritual lives of our families? What are we doing to help families continue to respond to God's word through the week?

3. What are our obstacles to nurturing family prayer and reflection on God's word in the home?

4. Are we providing the materials families need in order to support family prayer? What are we doing to help the families understand the use of leaflets that contain the Sunday readings adapted for children?

Chapter 14

RE-EVALUATING AND REFINING THE CELEBRATION

Evaluating—and re-evaluating—our celebrations with children is as much a priority as is preparing for them. Actually, we cannot really prepare well without careful evaluations. We learn not just by doing, but by reflecting on what we do—and by being attentive to both explicit and implicit "feedback." If you ask children to evaluate a celebration, they may not know how to respond. However, they can be very articulate about the quality of a celebration by the way they participate—or fail to participate. Even then, looks can be deceiving.

In one parish, the leaders thought an older boy was not terribly involved in the celebration—at least not by outward appearances. He was never disruptive. He simply hung around the outside of the group, leaned against the wall, showed little expression on his face. Although seemingly uninvolved, he actually was not missing a thing. Soon, he volunteered to be one of the "shepherds" for the younger children—to help them get settled and to sing the right words to the responses. He seemed to be "hanging out" until he found his place in the group.

We need to be careful about what standards we follow and how we apply those standards. While rituals follow patterns or "rules," ritual should not serve to control but to *liberate* the spirit. You may, for example, pick up the book of readings to proclaim the gospel when a child lets you know she has something to say that can't wait. If we are sensitive to such needs, we avoid sending children mixed messages about gathering in the presence of a *loving* God who—the children may conclude from our ignoring or hushing them—really does not care to listen to them. The *Directory*, again, applies a standard that we need to apply in our evaluations: do our celebrations serve the spiritual advantage of the children?

Different communities will celebrate differently, particularly communities whose cultural and ethnic backgrounds differ. The way a community of African-American children move in a procession or in response to the word proclaimed, for instance, may be quite different from the way an Anglo or Hispanic community might move and express a sense of reverent response. Within this context, and allowing for individuality in children and communities of children, we'll reflect upon a number of evaluation questions that you might follow in devising your own set of criteria for the particular community you are serving.

At the end of this chapter you will find a planning and evaluation form designed for use each week. If the leaders of the word use this form faithfully, you will begin to see a pattern emerge. This pattern will give you a picture of your celebrations that will serve as the basis of periodic general evaluation meetings, held perhaps every month or two. You might want to review your weekly planning/evaluation forms in light of the questions and reflections presented in this chapter. Our questions follow the order of events in the celebration.

1. *The Gathering Rites*

Is the leader of the Liturgy of the Word with children part of those who participate in the opening procession? Is the lectionary for children carried in the procession either by the leader or by the children? How are children represented in this processional? The principle here is: everyone who plays a role in the ritual should be part of those who walk in the opening procession.

2. *The Invitation to Celebrate the Word*

Does the presider take enough time so that the children have time to gather before he commissions the leader? With what words does the presider address the children and invite them to gather? Principle: the invitation and movement of the children should flow with the celebration, elevating the entire congregation's awareness and appreciation of God's own presence in the word.

3. *Procession with the Book of Readings*

Is the congregation joining in the "centering" song with the children? Does the procession reflect a natural—rather than an imposed—reverence and dignity? Is the mood celebrative? Are the song leaders spread throughout the procession? Are the older children helping the younger ones? Is the book of readings being carried respectfully, accompanied by children carrying lighted candles?

4. *Welcoming/Environment*

Is the room's lighting and furnishings arranged to convey a sense of sacred space? Does the available seating and arrangement of seating serve the varied needs of the group? How do the children arrange themselves upon entering the room? Does everyone feel at home in the entire group? Or do some children form their own separate sub-groups, older children from younger ones? Are the older teenage "shepherds" and other adults helping the children gather reverently? Are the adults truly a part of the worshiping community or have they become more like monitors than models? How effectively are the older children and adults serving as models in their movement, posture, prayerful attitude?

Are there strong singers or music leaders among those first in the room so that the processional music keeps the children focused on the celebration and shapes the mood of the gathering as children enter the room? If you do not use processional music in which the children sing, do you use instrumental music to create a prayerful mood as the children enter the room?

Is the book of readings held high while the children enter and then, after the children enter, reverently displayed in view of the children? Does the leader's placement of the book on the display stand convey a sense of respect for God's word? Does the setting in which the book is displayed convey a sense of God's presence in the word?

The principle here is: orchestrate the various elements and movements so as to solicit and awaken from within the children a sense of performing the ritual celebration, rather than managing their compliance to a prescribed behavior pattern.

5. *The First Reading*

Do the children sing a centering song before the reading; perhaps the refrain of the response?

If an introduction to the reading is necessary, is it done properly, avoiding preachy or didactic overtones?

Is the reader prepared? Does the reader wait until the children are settled and ready to listen? Are the children attentive and engaged? How are children who are distracted brought into focus on the reading? What led up to their distraction? Is the source of the distraction preventable in future gatherings?

Does the reader's style of delivery complement the literary style of the text? Is the reader sensitive to the children's non-verbal response while they are listening to the reading?

6. *Response*

Do the children sing rather than recite the response? Are the musical lines appropriately brief and the notation repetitive enough so that the children can pick up the words and melody without practicing? Are the words of the response displayed in large type so that children who can read are better able to participate?

Do the music leaders know the music well enough to avoid playing tape-recorded music during the celebration? Do the selected music and words complement the content of the reading?

Do the leaders incorporate gestures and body movements that involve the children? Do the children feel free to express themselves spontaneously? Are musical or rhythm instruments available for the children to use?

7. *Gospel Acclamation*

Do the children stand to sing the acclamation and to express respect for the proclamation (presence) of the Word of God? Does the movement of the celebration build as you reach and announce the gospel with the acclamation? Do the children enthusiastically sing rather than recite the acclamation? *When appropriate*, is the acclamation integrated or interspersed with the reading of the gospel so that the children are more actively involved in celebrating the proclamation?

8. *Gospel*

Is the reader prepared to proclaim the gospel with conviction and enthusiasm? *When appropriate*, are the children involved in a dramatic reading of the gospel narrative?

When the gospel is in story form, does the reader proclaim the text in a story-telling way? Is the reader attentive to how well the children are engaged in listening?

If a child wants to say something during the reading, does the reader acknowledge the child in such a way as to integrate the child's comment or question with the proclamation? Are the leaders skilled in recognizing a child wanting attention, even when the child may seem to be interrupting the celebration?

9. *Reflection on Readings*

Does the leader listen first to what the children have

heard God say to them? Does the leader avoid using God's word to teach doctrine or admonish the children about the way to behave? Is the leader's style sensitive to the creative power of God's word?

Do the children feel free to respond, secure in the knowledge that everyone will respect their reflections? Does the leader affirm the movement of God's Spirit in the children by celebrating their responses, perhaps by integrating the singing of the gospel acclamation or the refrain of the response with the children's reflections?

10. *Profession of Faith*

Is the creed adapted to the children's understanding? Is its basic form Trinitarian? Are the variations sensitive to the content of the Sunday's readings and complementary to the liturgical season? Has the leader personalized the creed by integrating with the creed what the children heard God say to them? Rather than a recital of doctrinal beliefs, is the creed a prayerful response of the children to God's word?

11. *Prayer of the Faithful*

Does the prayer of the faithful complement the content of the Sunday's readings? Does the prayer rise from the children and express their concerns?

12. *Return of Children to the Main Assembly*

Is the ending of the children's liturgy coordinated with the ending of the main assembly's Liturgy of the Word? Does the congregation make the children feel welcome? Is the return of the children orderly and respectful?

Family Involvement

Do parents and other family members participate on occasion in the children's Liturgy of the Word? What form of support is the parish providing to help parents prayerfully reflect on and respond to God's word through the week at home? Are leaflets containing the Sunday readings adapted for children distributed to families as they leave the church? Are families encouraged through pulpit and parish bulletin notes to use the leaflets at home?

Communication with Parishioners

As with any parish activity, communication with parishioners is vital. Often parents and other parishioners do not have a clear understanding of what the Liturgy of the Word with children is about. One parish leader reported that after mass one Sunday a parent asked, "What are you teaching my child about the mass when the children leave?" After the leader explained that the purpose was not to teach *about* the mass but to enrich the children's celebration and participation in mass, the parent responded, "In that case, I don't want my child to participate."

Often negative comments from parents are products of misunderstanding. Aside from having celebrations of the word with children that are intergenerational, it is helpful for parents to taste and see what the children are experiencing. Such exposure will help parents begin to appreciate the difference between children's liturgies and catechetical instruction. Moreover, when parents do understand, they can more intelligently evaluate the quality of the children's liturgies and provide the leaders with helpful suggestions based on their children's reactions and responses at home.

Some parishioners may find the procession out of the main assembly or the children's return a distraction. Again, such reactions may come from a lack of understanding and appreciation for the need to recognize children as having the right to celebrations that benefit their spiritual lives. On the other hand, these same parishioners frequently have creative suggestions for improving celebrations. Therefore, evaluation and planning meetings of the ministry team should be announced in the parish bulletin and open to all parishioners. The liturgy is the work not just of the ministry team but of all the people.

Moreover, the evaluation of the children's liturgy by the entire parish is an important step in awakening all parishioners to their responsibility to the children. The flip-side of this responsibility is a welcome opportunity—a chance to improve the celebration of the word for the entire assembly. Could this be another blessing in disguise?

Is it stretching Isaiah's point to mention his prophetic remark: "A little child will lead us to the reign of God"? Certainly it is not stretching Jesus' point: "Do not keep the children from me. For it is to such as these that the reign of God belongs" (*Mark* 10:14). What more can we say?

It's God's word.

Discussion Questions

1. How can we establish a set of criteria for evaluating our celebrations of the word with children?

2. How can we establish a pattern of regular evaluations?

3. Follow the questions raised in the chapter concerning each part of the celebration. Design an evaluation form that takes into account the local parish circumstances and the needs of the children.

4. How can we improve and make available the resources needed to help parents and leaders improve their skills and deepen their knowledge of the scriptures, liturgy, the spirituality of children and to nourish their own spirituality?

Bibliography & Resources

Note: This listing of publications includes both basic documents and materials that will help you implement the celebration of the word with children. While these materials come from a variety of publishers, they are available through a single source (prices subject to change):

Treehaus Communications, Inc.
P.O. Box 249
Loveland, Ohio 45140
(800) 638-4287
Fax: (513) 683-2882

CIC UPDATE
The Christian Initiation of Children Newsletter
The CIC UPDATE Newsletter is published four times a year. Its purpose is to keep readers informed of developments in the Christian initiation of children, particularly as envisioned by the RCIA and the *Directory for Masses With Children.* You can receive CIC UPDATE through individual or bulk subscriptions. For complete information contact Treehaus Communications, Inc. (800) 638-4287.

The Rite of Christian Initiation of Adults
Study Edition
The complete text of the rite together with additional rites approved for use in the dioceses of the United States of America. The order for the Christian initiation of children is an integral part of the RCIA and the context within which the Christian initiation of children is to function.
396 pp. LTP/1988 ISBN 0-930467-94-9 $8.00

The Directory for Masses With Children
This document provides the official guidelines for eucharistic celebrations with children as well as for celebrations of the word with children at gatherings attended largely by adults. The *Directory* is essential reading for those who want to enrich children's worship. It is concerned with all the ways of initiating children into full and active participation in the liturgical life of the church. Its perspective is broad and its guidelines practical.
24 pp. USCC/1973 ISBN 1-55586-291-8 $1.95

The Liturgy Documents: A Parish Resource
The most important and useful documents of the liturgical reform are collected here: *Constitution on Sacred Liturgy*; the *General Instruction on the Roman Missal*, the introduction to the *Lectionary for Masses*; *General Norm for the Liturgical Year and the Calendar*; the *Directory for Masses With Children*; *Environment and Art in Catholic Worship; Fulfilled in Your Hearing* (about the Sunday homily); *This Holy and Living Sacrifice* (rationale and norms for distributing communion under both species), and excerpts from the *Ceremonial of Bishops* (many principles applicable to parish celebrations). With review and brief commentary.
400 pp. LTP/1991 ISBN 0-929650-46-8 $9.95

The Church Speaks About Sacraments With Children
This brief volume contains excerpts from basic church documents related to the Christian initiation of children. Mark Searle provides an illuminating commentary that will help pastoral leaders formulate guidelines for the initiation of children.
66 pp. LTP/1990 $4.50

Issues in the Christian Initiation of Children:
Catechesis & Liturgy
Edited by Kathy Brown and Frank C. Sokol, this volume draws on the experience of various contributors in

dealing with central questions posed by the *Rite of Christian Initiation of Adults* as it affects the initiation of children.
219 pp. LTP/1989 ISBN 0-930467-97-3 $7.95

Sharing our Biblical Story
Revised Edition
    Joseph P. Russell has written an idea book for religious educators and parents that shows how to base Christian education on the Bible stories that occur in the context of worship. This book focuses on biblical stories from each of the three cycles (with variations in readings as they appear in the lectionaries of different denominations), provides background material and offers suggestions for emphasis.
346 pp. Morehouse-Barlow/1988 ISBN 0-8192-1425-6 $19.95

Children's Liberation: A Biblical Perspective
    Relatively little has been written about children in the Bible, especially about the primacy given to them in the gospel of Jesus. This enlightening volume provides rich insights into understanding that unless we are as children, we will not enter the reign of God. By scripture scholar, Joseph A. Grassi.
128 pp. Liturgical Press/1991 $5.95

The Spiritual Life of Children
    Robert Coles, professor of psychiatry and medical humanities at Harvard University, has spent 30 years listening to children around the world and is one of the most respected contributors of our time to our understand- ing of the culture of children. In this book, Dr. Coles shows us children face to face with the idea of God, in whose presence they seem to be fearless. Children discourse on the nature of God's wishes, on the devil, heaven and hell, faith and skepticism. Recommended for parents as well as parish leaders.
378 pp. Houghton Mifflin/1991 ISBN 0-395-55999-5 $10.95

The Children's God
David Heller, a clinical psychologist, interviewed forty children of four different religious backgrounds (Jewish, Catholic, Baptist, and Hindu) about God. Though he finds some differing views attributable to age, gender, and religious background, he discovers to a surprising degree a common vision of God that cuts across ethnic and religious differences.
151 pp. Univ. of Chicago Press/1986 ISBN 0-226-32636-5 $8.95

The Religious Potential of the Child
Second English Edition
This book describes an experience with children from ages three to six, an experience of adults and children dwelling together in the mystery of God. Author Sofia Cavalletti offers a glimpse into the religious life of the atrium, a specially prepared place for children to live out their silent request: "Help me come closer to God by myself." Preface by Mark Searle.
248 pp. LTP/1992 ISBN 0-929650-67-0 $12.95

Children, Liturgy, and Music
Edited by Virgil C. Funk, this book of 15 articles combines theological expertise with pastoral experience to help your parish implement the *Directory for Masses With Children.*
136 pp. The Pastoral Press/1990 ISBN 0-912405-73-2 $9.95

The Christian Initiation of Children: Hope for the Future
Robert D. Duggan and Maureen A. Kelly provide a challenging vision and practical suggestions for restructuring parish religious education practices to complement the implementation of the *Rite of Christian Initiation of Adults.* An excellent description of the convergence of liturgy and catechetics and its ramifications for shaping the future church.
138 pp. Paulist Press/1991 ISBN 0-8091-3258-3 $6.95

The SUNDAY Handbook for Ministers of the Word
A practical resource for every minister of the word—
provides methodology a well as an overview of biblical texts
and liturgical seasons. Developed under the direction of
Christiane Brusselmans.
32 pp. w/pocket cover Treehaus/1989 ISBN
0-929496-06-X $7.95

SUNDAY Lectionary for Children
The Sunday lectionary adapted for children, endorsed
for liturgical use by the Canadian Conference of Catholic
Bishops, features: inclusive language, large type, lines of
text end to complement natural speaking breaks, adapted
in keeping with the *Directory for Masses With Children*,
handsomely bound for use in celebrations of the word.
Year A, B, and C in separate volumes. Developed under
the direction of Christiane Brusselmans with Sr. Paule
Freeburg, D.C., Rev. Edward Matthews, Christopher
Walker.
172 pp. Treehaus/1991-92 ISBN 0-929496-38-8 (Year A);
ISBN 0- 929496-57-4 (Year B); ISBN 0-929496-91-4 (Year C)
$29.95 each when purchased in a set ($49.95 individually)

SUNDAY Leader's Weekly Guide
Each volume covers 52 Sundays and special feasts.
Each celebration features: 1) Focus of the Readings; 2)
Ideas for Reflecting on the Readings with Children; 3) the
Sunday readings adapted for children; 4) Music for
Responses and Gospel Acclamations; 5) Prayer of the Day.
Also features Background to the Sunday Readings and
Liturgical Seasons as well as Planning & Evaluation Form.
Developed under the direction of Christiane
Brusselmans with Sr. Paule Freeburg, D.C., Rev. Edward
Matthews, Christopher Walker.
178 pp. Treehaus/1990-93 ISBN 0-929496-93-0 (Year A);
ISBN 0- 929496-58-2 (Year B); ISBN 929496-92-2 (Year C)
$29.95 each when purchased in set of 3. ($49.95
individually.) Contact Treehaus for bulk discounts.

SUNDAY Family Leaflets

These four-page and six-page weekly leaflets are for use at home or school after the Sunday celebration. They feature: the Sunday readings adapted for children ages 5 to 12 years; picture-story illustrations of the readings; prayers; and description of biblical people and places. Essential for family involvement and continued reflection on the word at home.

Weekly / Treehaus / Call (800) 638-4287 for bulk rates & discounts.

MY SUNDAY SHEPHERD
Family Leaflets

These full-color seasonal leaflets are for families with children 3 to 5 years old. Designed to help the young child take those first steps—hand-in-hand with parents—in celebrating the gospel story on Sunday and responding in praise throughout the week. *My Sunday Shepherd* initiates the young child gradually into the liturgical life of the church through a prayerful family life. Each leaflet features a story-picture of the Sunday gospel on one side and, on the other side, a prayer guide that helps parents pray in a way that enables their children to pray with them and to respond to God's word throughout the week. Set of 8 leaflets and 1 Parent Guide for each of the following seasons: Advent/Christmas; Lent/Easter Sunday; Eastertide/Pentecost.

Weekly during these seasons / Treehaus / Call (800) 638-4287 for subscription information and bulk discounts.

SUNDAY Scripture Response Posters

A complete series of 53 beautiful posters (17 x 22 inches), designed to be decorated or colored by leaders, helpers, or parents, for use during the celebration of the word. Each poster features the enlarged text of Responses and Gospel Acclamations and a large picture-story illustration of the Sunday scriptures. Especially helpful

for younger children. Available for all three cycles, Year A, B, and C.
Weekly / Treehaus / Call (800) 638-4287 for prices and discounts.

How to Celebrate the Word With Children...and Why
Video
  Features a demonstration celebration with commentary by Father Edward Matthews, one of the primary authors of the *Directory for Masses With Children.*
30 minutes with guide / Treehaus /1990 $49.95

SUNDAY: A Basic Celebration Resource
Video
  A video "dictionary" for the SUNDAY Celebration of the Word material, hosted by Christiane Brusselmans and Gerard A. Pottebaum. Each element of the SUNDAY Celebration of the Word material is defined, along with its uses. An important tool for any parish developing liturgies that respect the spiritual life of children.
21 Minutes / Treehaus /1990 $19.95

Lectionary for Masses and Other Celebrations With Children
  In 1991 the United States bishops approved a *Lectionary for Masses With Children*, a translation by the American Bible Society (Contemporary English Version-CEV). After confirmation by the Holy See, this lectionary will be published and authorized for use in Fall 1993.
  There will be a single volume for each year of the three-year cycle (plus major feast days) and a separate volume for weekdays. Several publishers will be publishing their own editions. While not available as we go to press, these volumes may be ordered through Treehaus Communications, Inc. Prices are still to be determined. Call (800) 638-4287 for information.

Planning & Evaluation Form

PLANNING

Sunday _____ Cycle _____

CELEBRATION OF THE WORD

Centering song or music _____

Welcome *(Inspired by focus of readings)*: _____

Readings:

First_____ Reader _____

Responsorial Psalm _____ Singer _____

Refrain _____ Singer _____

Gospel Acclamation _____ Singer _____

Gospel_____ Reader _____

Special Activities *(Dramatization, reading in parts, Bible song, environment, etc.)*:_____

_____

Reflections on Readings Notes: _____

_____

Creed: _____

Prayer of the Faithful: _____

Response:_____

Suggestions for Intentions:_____

Symbolic Actions *(Including special rites, preparation of banners, key biblical or liturgical words or sentences on posters or scrolls.)*:

_____

_____

EVALUATION

1. Review of the celebration. _____

_____

2. Evaluation. _____

     What went well: _____

     _____

     What needs improvement:_____

     _____

3. Action required for the future. _____

_____

_____

_____

(You may enlarge and duplicate this page.)